1046   7/6

THE NELSONIAN LIBRARY

"LET'S GO CLIMBING!"

No. 65

THE SUB-CNEIFION RIB.

Crossing a slab to the arête.   The lake below is Llyn Idwal.

" Let's Go Climbing ! "

by

C. F. KIRKUS

Illustrated with Photographs
and a Map

THOMAS NELSON AND SONS LTD
LONDON EDINBURGH PARIS MELBOURNE
TORONTO AND NEW YORK

First published February 1941
Reprinted 1946

CONTENTS

ILLUSTRATIONS

"LET'S GO CLIMBING!"

Chapter I

WHY DO WE CLIMB?

IT was cold and bleak when I reached the summit of Snowdon at 5.30 on Easter Sunday morning.

I had been climbing all Saturday, and had returned in the evening to the little climbers' hut in the Ogwen Valley, where I was staying. Most of the others were drifting off to their bunks, but it was such a lovely night—starlit and frosty—that it was more than I could resist. So I collected a little food, pulled on my sodden boots, found my ice-axe, balaclava helmet and gloves, and set off, a little after midnight, with a strange feeling of high adventure.

It was wonderful to be walking across the crackly frozen bog, all alone in the night. I experienced a satisfying sense of freedom and all sleepiness was driven away by the keen air; I felt I could keep going for ever.

Soon I reached a slope of hard snow and had to cut some steps. I cut with a steady rhythm, and got very hot and sticky with the hard exercise. It was almost as light as day, with the moonlight on the snow, and I had no difficulty at all in seeing where I was going, until I got into the shadow. Then a kind of chill seemed to descend on me and all the snow looked even and featureless.

I had a short rest when I reached the crest of the rounded eastern ridge of the Glyders and then set off on the 1,500-foot descent to Pen-y-Pass. It was very rough and stony, and the moonlight played queer tricks. I would step on to a firm-looking rock and find it was a deep hole, or else I would prepare to jump down a drop of four feet, only to be brought up with a jolt after a few inches. After a little practice you learn to take up these shocks in your knees, so that you can run quite safely, even in the dark, down a steep rough slope, without any danger of a sprained ankle. The fact that you are wearing heavy climbing-boots instead of shoes makes a great difference, of course.

I passed by Llyn Cwm-y-ffynnon, a beautiful little tarn, now half frozen over, and reached Pen-y-Pass (the top of the Pass of Llanberis) at about 3 a.m. It was quite an eerie business, climbing over the rickety stone wall with all the caution of a cat-burglar, so as not to arouse the sleeping occupants of the hotel. My nailed boots made a loud ringing sound as I crossed the main road and set foot on the Snowdon massif, which was my objective.

The rest of the expedition was pure joy. I

SNOWDON AT EASTER.

made my way, first along the crazy path and up grass slopes, and then up slopes of snow where sometimes I had to cut a few steps. Then came the rocks, a mere scramble in summer-time and not difficult even now, though they were glazed with ice in places. And finally a narrow snowy ridge brought me to the summit of Crib Goch.

Crib Goch is in many ways the most lovely peak of Snowdon. It is just over 3,000 feet in height, and from Pen-y-Pass appears as a sharp cone. But on the other side is a narrow ridge, which is justly famous among mountain-lovers. I shall never forget crossing the ridge this Easter morning. The hard snow was piled up to a knife-edge on the crest, while on the right it dropped in an almost vertical wall of white. The slope on the left was easier, but still quite steep. The snowless valleys were almost invisible, so that there was nothing to be seen in front but this narrow gleaming moonlit edge, dropping down into nothingness. I felt as though I was poised in the air, on the very top of the world.

All around were snowy summits, dropping weirdly into the inky blackness beneath; they looked almost like clouds. Yet there was no atom of danger to take my mind off all this magnificence; I knew the place well and felt perfectly at home.

I was feeling warm and exhilarated as I made my way through this enchanted scene, over the spiky pinnacles and up the rocky ridge of Crib-y-ddisgyl, and on to y Wyddfa, the summit of

Snowdon. It was 5.30 now and beginning to get light. The moon seemed to have lost its brilliance, and the snow was a dead unearthly white, cold and spectral. A chilly wind had sprung up and I shivered as I forced my way into the old wooden hut on the summit. The door was jammed with frozen snow and it was a tight squeeze to get in.

There was no furniture inside nor glass in the windows, and the floor was covered with a thick sheet of ice. I ate a little food, but my fingers got frozen as soon as I took off my gloves, so I just stamped my feet and shivered and waited for the sunrise.

The east window was almost covered by a framework of feathery icicles, and I kept watch through a ragged hole that was left in the middle. All the valleys were filled with mist, with the peaks standing up clear above, like islands. It got slowly lighter, but no warmer. Then presently a scarlet glow appeared above a level purple bank of cloud lying on the horizon, and soon the red sun, looking queerly oval, came into view. As soon as it rose above the cloud it changed to gold and made the icicles in the window gleam like diamonds. I could feel its warmth immediately and grew cheerful and comfortable again in an instant.

Half an hour later I was descending to Glaslyn in a sweltering heat, the great snowy bowl of the cwm acting as a kind of giant reflector.

I have begun with this description to try and let you feel something of the spirit of the mountains.

If you are keen you can manage an expedition like this after a very short time. You must first get used to being on the mountains by yourself, and learn to find your way in a mist. Then you must practise some rock-scrambling until you feel really at home on craggy ridges. There is nothing very alarming about mountaineering on a moonlit night, but the snow-climbing is not so quickly learnt ; until you have mastered the rudiments of this branch of the sport it will be as well to have an experienced companion with you on winter expeditions.

And now—why do we go climbing ? I hope I have already succeeded in showing you something of the attraction. Most of you must sometimes have felt an urge to get away for a little while from all the noise and bustle of modern civilization, to escape into wild country quite away from other people, where you are your own master and where everything that you do depends on yourself and on yourself alone. It is the same feeling that makes desert islands sound so attractive. We cannot all go to desert islands—and might not like them if we did—but we can do the next best thing and go to the mountains.

Then there is the scenery. If you have been used only to woods and trees and fields, you will be amazed when you get among the mountains. There you will see great cliffs and rocky ridges, and tarns nestling in lonely hollows, and the valleys so far below will seem to belong to another world. It is impossible to describe this spirit of the mountains, but you will feel its spell as soon as you are amongst them.

But we can get all this by just walking up, you may say. Why go out of your way to climb difficult rocks ? That is quite a sound argument, which is partly why I am going to tell you in the first few chapters what to do to make yourself a competent fell-walker. If you feel perfectly contented once you have learnt to wander safely over the homeland hills, and have no ambition to try anything harder, then it would be foolish to try to persuade you to climb against your will. You will have found a wonderful new world and a freedom that cannot be obtained elsewhere.

But there still remains the question—why do we climb ? The primary cause is, I think, the spirit of adventure. Fell-walking is a pleasant recreation, whilst climbing is a definite sport, fascinating and absorbing, and with a very special technique of its own. Perhaps, when you are resting half-way up a mountain, lazily basking in the sunshine, you may look across at a near-by precipice and amuse yourself by idly planning an imaginary route up the middle. At first it looks very hopeless and terrifying and inaccessible, and then you notice that there are quite a lot of grass ledges dotted about here and there. Then you see that these ledges are quite close together, and realize that the bits of steep rock separating them are actually quite short. Thus, in your mind, you have transformed an unclimbable cliff into a series of short rock walls. You have begun to acquire the mentality of the rock-climber. And it will be a further comfort if you realize that some of the ledges may be as big as rooms, and that the rocks which look so smooth from a distance are covered with holds and rough enough to remove the seat of your trousers if you give them a chance.

Then you may see a minute figure moving steadily up the steepest and sheerest part of the crag, with two others standing almost motionless on a ledge below, joined to the leader by the thin white line of the climbing-rope. And if you feel a momentary half-fearful desire to be with them, out there on the face of the cliff, then you are cut out to be a climber.

Then, perhaps, you race up to the summit, to be there in time to greet the victorious party. But instead of appearing with the strained anxious faces of people who have narrowly survived a great ordeal, they stroll up casually, carrying coils of rope, smoking pipes, and chatting cheerily. They assure you it is quite an easy climb and say they aren't expert enough to do anything difficult.

The lesson to be learnt from this is that you should not judge by appearances. Crags almost always look more difficult from a distance, especially if seen face-on, when a slope of easy angle may appear to be quite vertical.

Apart from what we may call its poetic appeal, climbing is a splendid sport. When people ask me why I climb, I ask them in return why they play rugger or tennis or cricket or hockey, or whatever games they do play. And almost invariably they argue that in other games you play to win, by pitting your strength and skill against the opposing team. But so you do in climbing, the only difference being that, in place of human opponents, you have to fight against the natural difficulties of the rocks themselves. Instead of playing another team you do a different climb ; instead of playing a return match you do the same climb again under different weather conditions. And if you don't believe that there is anything in climbing as exhilarating as dashing over the line to score a try or hitting a cricket ball for six, then you will soon alter your views if you give climbing a trial. To be poised on a steep smooth face, concentrating with every nerve, and then to stretch cautiously up and to come unexpectedly on a large handhold which solves the problem—that seems to be the most thrillingly satisfying moment of your life each time it happens.

But what about the danger, you may ask. Is it worth the risk ?

The answer to this is that climbing is not a dangerous sport if you follow the rules. People who take risks are not considered heroes in the climbing world ; they are considered fools and bad climbers. But when an accident does happen the newspapers make a terrific sensation of it : they give more prominence to the two or three fatal accidents that occur each year in this country than to a hundred motoring accidents. And that is why the general public regards climbing as a hazardous pastime. But if you always turn back when in doubt there should be very little danger. And if you do make a mistake and fall off, you have quite a good chance of being held by your second man if the rope is being managed correctly. And the second can fall off to his heart's content, with no injury except to his pride (some seconds seem to have none) and a certain tenderness—well deserved —about the ribs.

There is little doubt that climbing is much less dangerous than, say, motor-cycling or aviation ; you will be able to realize this better when you have learnt the use of the rope and seen the very adequate precautions that are adopted.

As an exercise climbing is unrivalled, since every muscle in the body is used. It teaches judgment and courage and coolness in emergency, and makes you forget completely all the worries of everyday life. It is a wonderful chance for adventure in pure air and magnificent surroundings. Few who start climbing ever give it up. Once a climber, always a climber.

CHAPTER II

BEGINNINGS

MOUNTAINS have always been in my blood. Some people have a passion for the sea, but for me it was the mountains that called. Luckily my parents have similar tastes, so that I did not have to endure the all too usual seaside holiday ; horrible pictures of crowded beaches and bathing tents and gaudy ice-cream stalls come into my mind. I am afraid that in certain ways I was a wretched little snob in those days, looking down with scorn on all who were content with a normal holiday. I conveniently ignored the fact that young children and old people might not be able to disport themselves among the hills, and of course it never entered my head that any one who had no desire to climb a mountain was worthy of the slightest attention. I am more tolerant now and thankful that people do go to the seaside and leave the mountains free.

I ascended my first mountain at the age of seven—a rocky 2,000-foot lump called Manod, near Ffestiniog (in Wales, it is hardly necessary to add). That was a great day in my life, and ever afterwards I gazed at all mountains with longing. I was not content to laze about in the valleys ; I was itching to be on the summits. I can still remember my tears of rage and disappointment when my father refused to take me up Moelwyn because there was cloud on the top. I thought he showed a very poor and unadventurous spirit.

Then came the great day when I made the ascent of Snowdon, at the age of nine. We went up by Glaslyn, and I was thrilled beyond words. It was very hot and I can remember the cold crystal-clear springs that I felt certain had saved my life on the laborious but, to me, entrancing zigzags. It was wonderful to be at last actually on a slope composed entirely of rocks, surrounded by terrific precipices that exceeded my wildest expectations. I had provided myself with a stout and knobbly stick, which I had cut myself with loving care ; it had rather the appearance of a petrified snake or a giant corkscrew. But in my eyes it was an indispensable companion, and I decided that some young men we saw coming down at breakneck speed without sticks of any kind must be very ignorant of mountain-craft. The whole day was one orgy of continuous rapture which I have never since been able quite to recall.

Two years later there was another thrill, when with great trepidation we crossed the knife-edge ridge of Crib Goch. I must have presented a queer spectacle, with a canvas tea-bag in one hand—for we could not dream of doing without our 4 o'clock tea—and a walking-stick in the other.

We used to spend our summer holidays at

Carrog, in the Vale of Llangollen, and before I was twelve years of age I was allowed to wander over the mountains on my own. This shows the value of training one's parents from the very earliest age. I found that, properly managed, they gave very little trouble.

I walked over the Berwyns in all weather and learnt to find my way in mist by map and compass. I even tried some rock-climbing. There is a broken slaty cliff on the eastern side of the highest summits of the Berwyn range, and I lured my two younger brothers there on a stormy day of cloud and wind and hail. I had thoughtfully provided myself with a clothes-line, for which I had paid the large sum of eightpence. (It broke later when I was trying to pull my brother up a haystack.)

We traversed across the slope to the foot of the steepest-looking buttress of rock I could find. My brothers naturally objected—one was only eleven years old—but I assured them that this was the easiest and in fact the only route, and that they had better follow me if they wished to escape with their lives. Luckily the cloud hid the simple gullies on either side from view. So up they had to come, wet and cold and thoroughly miserable, up the loose muddy rock, with the cloud swirling round. Fortunately the clothes-line—we had only thirty feet for the three of us—did not choose this occasion to break. And when we reached the top, blue with cold, I took out a wet and battered thermometer and solemnly informed them that the temperature was 38 degrees Fahrenheit. This item of news was received with no great enthusiasm.

The following Christmas I was given *British Mountain Climbs*, a climbing guide-book, and this fired me with enthusiasm to do some real rock-climbing. So I purchased a proper climbing-rope, or rather line, guaranteed to hold nearly three-quarters of a ton and not to break on haystacks. And I nailed my boots with hobnails, putting them close together round the edge to make them look as much as possible like real climbing-boots.

Next summer a school friend was staying at Cynwyd, about five miles away from Carrog, and we used to cycle together to the Arans, which involved fifty miles cycling, apart from the walking and climbing. We found some nice, wet strenuous gullies, which had probably only been climbed a few times before, and enjoyed ourselves immensely. The Arans are nearly 3,000 feet in height and very wild and lonely ; we usually did not see a soul the whole day. But I was not very popular with my friend's parents, since he used to arrive back at all hours of the night. Unfortunately they were not such well-trained parents as mine ; he had not taken them in hand early enough.

When I was nearly seventeen, and had just left school, I managed to persuade the family to vary their usual routine and go to Bettws-y-Coed—a special concession because it was to be my last holiday before going to business. It seemed like heaven to me—only ten miles away from Snowdon and the Carnedds and the Glyders—on the doorstep of all the best climbing in Wales, in fact.

I spent practically the whole of this holiday in continuously breaking a rule that is being constantly hammered into beginners—climbing alone while still a novice. But what else could I do ? I did not know any climbers, and it was only occasionally that I could get my father or brothers to accompany me. There was only one alternative—not to climb— and that was unthinkable. The ambition of my life at that time was to do some recognized rock-climbs ; not just casual little scrambles, but real routes that had names and were described in the guide-book.

Though wrong as a policy, this early solo climbing taught me an immense amount. I knew that if I made a mistake I had no one to help me ; I had to rely entirely on my own skill and my own judgment. Thus, after a few sobering adventures which I shall presently relate, I learnt to climb carefully and safely, even when I knew I had a good second man behind me.

British Mountain Climbs was my climbing Bible. But it had been written in the days when gullies were in fashion, when cragsmen were still afraid to venture on steep exposed faces. Therefore gullies at first took up rather more than a fair share of my climbing, and it was in one of these clefts that I had my first fall.

Now you will first of all want to know exactly what is a gully. Imagine you are looking at a large precipice. The face of it is not flat ; it is seamed by deep rifts, running the whole height of the crag. These rifts are called gullies, while the jutting masses of rock that separate the gullies from one another are known as buttresses. Now you will notice that the gullies are not nearly as steep as the buttresses, and you may think you can walk up quite simply. Let us imagine you decide to do this. You pick out a likely-looking gully and begin walking up. The walls of the ravine are very steep, but the bed of the gully is set at quite a gentle angle, probably with a little stream running down.

All goes well for a time, and you imagine you are in for an easy scramble. Then, a little way ahead, you notice a great boulder jammed across the gully, but imagine that you will get round it easily enough. You scramble up to it and begin to feel a little doubtful. You are standing in a cave some thirty feet high, the roof of which is formed by the boulder, fully twenty feet across, which completely spans the cleft. In a situation like this there are three possibilities : sometimes you can climb up the back of the cave and find a tunnel behind the boulder—it is usually a strenuous job squirming through ; sometimes it is possible to climb one of the walls or work out from the back of the cave on to the outside of the chockstone, as this type of boulder is called ; or if both these methods fail you may have to try to find a way round on one side or the other. But in any case it has not proved to be the easy job you expected.

On the occasion in question I had cycled the

23

ten miles from Bettws and then slogged for an hour-and-a-half across the grassy slopes of the Carnedds, over the saddle below Pen Helig, and down to the grand precipice of Craig yr Ysfa. My objective was the Arch Gully, which was classified as difficult, so I was all keyed-up for a great struggle. The lower pitches—pitches are the stretches of actual climbing between the easier sections—went quite easily, and I arrived at the foot of the 50-foot chief obstacle. This was a vertical, three-sided cleft, about a yard across and had scarcely any holds, or so it seemed to me. The only way to get up is to put the back against the right wall and the feet against the left. Then you have to raise one foot a few inches, then press with the palms of your hands on the wall behind until your back goes up a bit. This type of problem is known as a chimney ; it is strenuous but usually safe, since you are firmly wedged. You can quite easily practise this technique in an ordinary doorway at home.

It was drizzling and the chimney was streaming with water and made more slippery by a coating of thick green moss. However, I arrived quite safely underneath the small chockstones which closed up the top of the chimney and overhung a little. I reached up cautiously with one hand and felt about until I found a fine sharp hold. One hard arm-pull and a struggle, and with a gasp of triumph I landed at the top of my first difficult rock-climb. It was a very small triumph really, for there are three harder standards, but it seemed a notable victory to me.

I descended a moderate gully into the Amphitheatre, a magnificent hollow in the centre of the
cliff. Nothing easy would do for me in my exultant
state of mind, so I made a bee-line for B. Gully.
This has one very awkward pitch, a steep slimy
crack overhung by a smooth chockstone. It was
raining heavily now, and muddy water was dripping
down dismally on every side.

I climbed the crack with a good deal of difficulty
and felt for holds on the boulder above, hanging
backwards from one hand. It all seemed as smooth
as glass and my fingers were so cold that I had lost
all feeling in them. My supporting hand was getting
tired and I felt I must do something quickly. I
did. I scraped the mud out of a slight crevice on
top of the overhanging boulder and decided to make
it do. I let go with my left hand, my right hand
slipped numbly from the boulder, and before I had
time to think I found myself lying in the bed of
the gully.

My first feeling was one of pained surprise that
it should have been possible for me to have fallen
off. Then I wondered how many bones I had
broken, and found that I was completely uninjured.
Finally I was overcome by such a feeling of baffled
rage at being thus ingloriously beaten that I rushed
at the pitch again, like a mad bull at a gate.

The same thing happened again, only this time
I fell and slid about 30 feet and stopped dangerously
near the edge of the pitch below. I decided it was
quite time to stop.

It was a very chastened and rather shaky climber that made his way back to Bettws that evening. Needless to say I did not breathe a word of the affair to any one. It was a disgraceful secret, to remain locked in my guilty bosom.

It is very easy to discover the causes for this little mishap—over-confidence, inexperience, and complete lack of judgment. It was bad enough to fall off once, but to go and do it again in a spirit of reckless petulance was sheer madness and showed that I was not really fit to be a climber. In climbing, everything should be considered calmly, and each move carefully thought out beforehand. Still, the whole thing did me a great deal of good. It showed me my limitations, made me think a lot, and made me much more careful in future. It was lucky for me that the fates picked on a nice safe place to teach me a lesson.

Youthful spirits soon recover, and the buttresses of Tryfan made my spirits rise again. Instead of gloomy wet gullies I was climbing on beautiful silvery-grey rock, warm and dry, and very rough. Tryfan is a superb mountain, three-peaked and very grand and rugged. And the climbing, too, is ideal for novices. You can taste the joy of being in exposed places with good holds ; you can look down quite calmly over a drop of a few hundred feet if you have an arm round a rock as big as a milestone. The rough rock feels wonderfully safe and comforting under your fingers and your boots seem to grip anywhere. But the best feature of

Tryfan is that the climbs finish on the summit; you feel that you have really climbed a mountain. And at the summit are two 15-foot stones known as Adam and Eve. These are quite close together, and people sometimes jump across. I have done it once or twice, but I feel that you would look rather silly if you slipped and broke a leg here after safely doing a difficult climb.

My next adventure was on Idwal Slabs. These lie at the south end of Llyn Idwal, on the Glyders, and are quite unique in their way. Imagine a flat slab of rough rock, 400 feet long and about 300 feet wide. Then imagine the whole thing tilted up at an angle of 45 or 50 degrees, and you have the Idwal Slabs. There are no large ledges and the holds are very small. Yet the climbing is not difficult on the whole, because of the easy angle.

I went up the easiest route, the only way described in my guide-book, and found it very simple. This lies up a groove, well marked by the scratches of thousands of nailed boots, and it would really be quite difficult to fall down, though you would have a long slide if you did. In fact some friends of mine, becoming bored with ordinary methods, once descended the lower part of the climb head-first. The mountains were rather crowded that day, and the spectacle caused quite a lot of excitement. Seeing two climbers apparently hanging upside-down on the Slabs, people naturally thought there had been some very unusual type of accident and rushed to the spot from all sides.

They then had the disappointment of seeing the two human caterpillars arrive at the bottom safely, though very red in the face. Others have descended the Slabs head-first—but not purposely.

At the top of the Slabs is a 200-foot wall of steep rock, which provides climbing of a much higher standard. At this point I should have made my escape either to the left or to the right, on to easier ground ; but I did not realize this and tried to climb directly upwards. I got into a recess called the Javelin Gully, though I did not know what it was at the time ; in fact I had never heard of it. The rocks became steeper, and soon I reached a completely perpendicular section. I could just touch a flat ledge with my hands, but there were no footholds at all. I was standing in a little recess like a sentry-box and wondering what to do next. I had quite a good ledge for my feet, but as soon as I left it I felt horribly insecure.

I got my hands on to the ledge above and tried to pull up, scraping feverishly with my feet against the rock. I made the effort several times, but could get no farther. My arms were feeling tired and it needed more and more courage each time to leave the safety of my foothold.

I remembered my fall on the Carnedds and decided to return. It is lucky that I did, because the Javelin Gully is a severe climb that needs a good deal of strength as well as skill. In 1937 two climbers were killed here ; they fell, roped, to the bottom of the Slabs, 500 feet below. How it

THE FINAL CRACK OF THE DIRECT ROUTE,
GLYDER FACH.

Note the method of belaying. A leader once fell off the
higher part of this severe pitch and escaped uninjured.

happened remains a mystery ; there must have been some mismanagement of the rope. Probably the second was giving the leader a shoulder, instead of remaining safely tied on to the rock a little lower down. You will be able to understand this better when I have described the use of the rope in a later chapter.

I came down a little and saw a line of slightly nail-marked holds leading diagonally out to the left. The holds got smaller and smaller, and finally I seemed to have reached the end of all things. Here, to my surprise, I found a piton (an iron spike) driven into a crack. So some one had been here before !

This was the first time I had been in a really exposed situation, and I was very impressed. I was standing on a narrow foothold and below me the rock dropped nearly vertically for over 100 feet. Below that again were the 400 feet of the Slabs.

I realized that I was in a tight corner and would have to keep a cool head. I had the horrible feeling of being like a fly on a wall, without, unfortunately, being provided with a fly's wings. I would have given anything to have been able to float gently off into space.

The rock above looked terrifying. It was obviously far beyond my standard. Then I saw a spike of rock about 12 feet above me. If I could reach that, I thought, I might manage to get up ; it looked easier above.

Luckily I always carried my 80-foot length of

climbing-line about with me. I uncoiled it now, and after several attempts managed to lasso the spike, cowboy-fashion, taking care not to swing myself off into space whilst I was doing so. Then I tied myself on to the end of the rope, so that I could not fall beyond the little ledge. So far, so good !

Then I climbed up the rope and managed to reach the spike. It was large and comforting and I grasped it thankfully. But the next section above was still difficult ; the holds were very small and I funked it without the security of having the rope above me. So down the rope I slid. Then up and down again, several times. I swung the rope off the spike in disgust and decided to double it round the piton and slide down the face of the cliff. I was beginning to get a little desperate now. But the rope jammed behind the piton and would not run, besides not being long enough to reach easy ground. So I gave up that idea as well. I was growing really tired of this spot ; I seemed to have spent half my life on a two-inch foothold.

More lassoing, and I got the spike again. Now for a do-or-die attempt. I climbed quickly up the rope and attacked the rocks above before I had time to change my mind. The holds seemed minute but I did not dare to hesitate, and almost before I had time to realize it I was above the difficulty and safe at last. What a relief ! I had never before felt so thankful for anything. The whole experience was worth while just for the sheer elation I felt at that moment.

There is no moral to this story. I made no real mistake ; I avoided running into actual danger ; and I succeeded in escaping safely from a difficult situation. And I had a glorious day of climbing adventure.

The following winter I managed to join a well-known club, and the next summer, while staying at the club cottage in the Ogwen Valley, I ran into real danger through my habit of climbing solo.

I now had no difficulty in obtaining climbing companions, but this time it happened that I was on my own. I had an urge for exploration, and probably also wished to make a name for myself, so I decided to have a look at Craig Lloer, a crag above Ffynnon Lloer, a lonely little lake set deep in one of the wild hollows of Carnedd Dafydd. I picked on the West Buttress, the shortest but steepest of the three sections of the cliff. It was about 200 feet high and had never been climbed.

The main feature of the route I had planned was a sinister-looking crack, some 80 feet up. So the first thing to do was to find a way to the foot of this crack. Things started quite easily but grew much more difficult when I reached the airy crest of the buttress, overlooking the vertical wall that dropped dizzily into the depths of the gully on the left. I climbed straight up the steep edge and gained the sloping ledge at the bottom of the crack by a very awkward movement.

The crack was about 40 feet high and overhung at the top. It looked very difficult. I tied the rope round my waist, with the other end hanging free, and started up. The crack was just about wide enough to fit a boot, and I progressed chiefly by jamming my hands and feet. In places there were small chockstones jammed in the crack and these were a great help, though I had first to test them very carefully to make sure that they were firm.

After an exhausting struggle I arrived at the overhang. I felt tired, because when you are climbing a pitch that is really vertical the arms get no rest at all. And now I had the overhang to tackle, where my whole weight would come on my hands. There was a convenient little stone here, jammed firmly in the crack, and I threaded the whole length of my rope down behind it, hanging on meanwhile with my left hand only. Then I tied myself on to the chockstone and was able to rest my arms, hanging more or less bodily on the rope.

Before I started off again I untied the rope from the chockstone but still left it hanging down behind, hoping that it might jam and hold me if I did happen to fall off the next section. Then I started up the overhang. It was very strenuous, and I struggled frantically. Then, just at a crucial moment, my rucksack jammed in the crack. With a despairing effort I worked it off my shoulder and abandoned it, precious camera and all. Another blind struggle and I was up, surprised and relieved to find the rucksack still hanging over the other shoulder.

Conditions looked much easier above and I

continued gaily. There was an innocent-looking bulge ahead, and I got half-way up without thinking very much about it. Then I realized that it was much more difficult than it had seemed. I could see a good handhold a little higher and made rather a grab for it. That was all very well, but there were no footholds, so that I was hanging from my hands alone. There were no holds above and I could not descend. My arms were getting tired. I looked down and saw a sheer drop of nearly 200 feet below me. My arms were aching now and I felt that I could not hold on much longer. I just hung there and waited for the end. Then I got into a panic and made a sudden convulsive spring round the corner on the left, where my hands mercifully landed on a hold.

I count that as one of my narrowest escapes. It was a foolish affair, because I don't think it was really such a very difficult place. I made the mistake of acting first and thinking afterwards. Always remember that the strongest man cannot hang for long on his arms alone. So when you make an arm-pull, be sure that it will land you on a foothold where you can rest.

You will probably have noticed that in spite of all these narrow escapes I did not suffer any injury. You may think that the risks cannot have been so great as I have made them appear. Well, you are probably right. The danger seemed real enough, but that is one of the most noticeable points about climbing; you have all kinds of narrow squeaks, and yet nothing serious happens. You get all the thrilling sensations of danger without much real risk.

Still, inexperience does lead to more than half the nasty smashes that do occur, so I am going to try and show you how you can take up climbing without having any similar disturbing adventures. When I began I had no one to help or advise me, and I did not even know of any books that would tell me how to make a start.

Since those days I have taken many a novice up his first climb, so I can realize the difficulties of almost every type of beginner, from the ultra-adventurous to the super-cautious. I have always taken a kind of showman's delight in introducing the marvels of the mountains to my friends, and it has given me the most intense pleasure to see their enthusiasm increase by leaps and bounds. Now I want to do the same for you. I want to take you through the whole field of mountaineering, from the very beginning, so that you can share all the glorious experiences which have meant so much to me. It won't be tedious ; there is very little book-work to be learnt. You can just go as far as you like with it, until you have found your own level. And when you have found that level—whether it be modest fell-walking or the most difficult rock-and-ice work— you will never regret having become a mountaineer.

Chapter III

MOUNTAIN WALKING

POSSIBLY you may want to start on real rock-climbing straight away. Well, you can if you like, but you will make a much greater success of it if you learn the whole art of mountaineering from the very beginning. You will gain far more enjoyment as well.

There are many climbers who most certainly are not mountaineers. Perhaps they have already sampled motor-racing and flying, and want yet another thrill. So they persuade some friend to take them up a rock-climb, or perhaps the friend persuades them.

A man starting under such conditions is seldom a success. He may turn out to be a brilliant cragsman, but he has not got the right attitude of mind. He probably does not care much about the mountains themselves or the scenery ; he is interested mainly in the physical exercise and the spice of danger. So he loses three-quarters of the enjoyment from the very beginning. He soon begins to get bored, and to sustain the interest indulges in competitive climbing, which always means dangerous climbing. Even if he does not

35

have an accident he loses interest after a year or two.

But if you set out to know the mountains you will learn to love them, and it will be quite a different tale. You will be happy just to be amongst them, whether you are tackling a hard or an easy climb, or merely wandering freely over the tops.

What must you do, then, to become a complete mountaineer ?

Firstly, you must learn to find your way in all weather over unknown tracts of mountainous country. Then you must gain proficiency in rock-climbing and snow-climbing. When you have done that you are ready for a visit to the Alps, under expert guidance.

But a holiday abroad is beyond the scope of many, in which case British climbing can be made an end in itself. In fact, there are many people who prefer it to Alpine climbing. The " very severe " climbs in this country are far harder than anything you would meet on an ordinary Alpine peak. But there is no need to follow the example of some Alpinists, usually poor climbers, who affect to despise the more difficult homeland routes and refer to them as " rock-gymnastics." It must be remembered that many of those who have done most brilliantly on Everest have been experts on British rock.

Climbers quite often successfully finish their climb and then lose their way walking down in the cloud, and land up in the wrong valley. They have

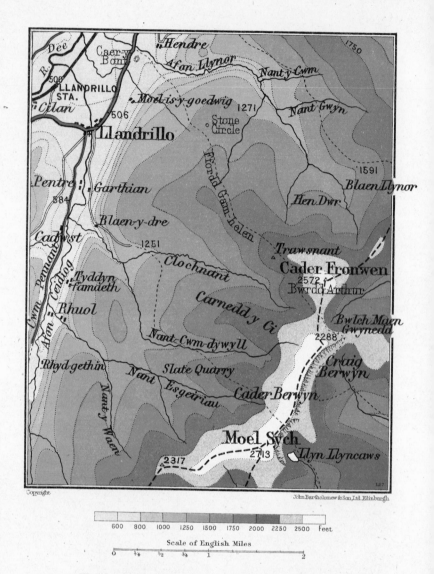

THE BERWYNS, NORTH WALES

a long walk back, which serves them right; but they may also cause a great deal of anxiety by their non-arrival, and search parties may be sent out. So it is well worth while, from this aspect alone, to learn something about the art of route-finding, especially since it is such a simple matter.

No elaborate equipment is needed for mountain-walking in summer. Any old clothes will do—grey flannel bags or plus-fours, or shorts if it is warm, golf-stockings, an open shirt, sports jacket or golf-jacket, and a spare sweater or pullover. On a hot day the jacket may seem to be unnecessary, but its pockets are a great boon.

The same sort of clothing will do for girls or ladies. Skirts are unsatisfactory for scrambling and hopeless for climbing, though possible for straight-forward walking. Special climbing-breeches are made for ladies, but ordinary " slacks," tucked inside the stockings at the ankle, will meet the case. Many a woman climber has made a start in a borrowed pair of men's trousers.

The feminine point of view will insist, of course, on an outfit that looks fairly presentable. What usually happens is that something light and smart is worn at the outset, whilst the heavier and less becoming spares that may be needed on the summits are carried up in the rucksack of the long-suffering male companion.

The most important item still remains—footwear. Climbing-boots, of course, are ideal, but there is no need to postpone your ramble just because you have not got them. However, you may as well get them as soon as possible, since they are absolutely necessary for climbing. In any case boots are better than shoes, but either will do with a few hobnails knocked in. There is danger of sprained ankles going over rough ground in shoes.

Gloves are useful, and leather mitts are warmer than woollen ones. Also, a balaclava helmet or a scarf to tie over the ears is often a great comfort. Of course, the weather conditions must be taken into account ; you won't need all this clothing in a heat-wave. But you must remember that it is likely to be colder higher up ; it may be very close and muggy in the valley, but conditions are very different on a high ridge, with a blustery wind blowing the cold rain into your face. So take some spare clothes with you. But you can learn only by experience. Many times will you sweat and many times will you shiver, before you manage to strike the happy mean. It is all part of the fun.

There is one golden rule to remember : always take plenty of food with you. Fatigue and cold become very dangerous when you are short of food. Meat or ham sandwiches are good, and tomato or cucumber keeps them moist and refreshing. Always take some chocolate or sweets as a reserve, because anything that contains sugar is very sustaining. There is no point in carrying anything to drink, since you are sure to come across plenty of streams. However, an orange is often very welcome when you are on a ridge, away from water. In short, take any food you like which is not too bulky and is easily carried. A crushed jam tart or cream trifle is never very appetizing when it has to be sucked off a dirty sock. It is also rather unpleasant putting on a shirt that is lined with mouldy banana.

A thermos flask of hot tea is very stimulating, if any noble soul can be found to carry it, but it is doubtful if it is worth its weight. You will probably find you have rather a lot to carry at first, but you will soon learn what to take and what to leave behind.

You will now need a rucksack (not a knapsack). Get a small one, with two or three outside pockets, and make sure that it is waterproof. Leather shoulder-straps are better than webbing, but this is not a very important point for small weights. Before the war you could buy a satisfactory article for five shillings or so. If one sack is carried for every two people, it should not weigh more than ten or twelve pounds when loaded. So many people set off on a day's outing looking as though they were going to be away for a month, pressing on with grim determined faces and trying not to wish they had never started.

You may have noticed that I have made no mention of raincoats. They just are not worth while. They are a nuisance to carry and are a hindrance in walking and scrambling. If the weather is really bad you will get wet whatever you wear, and it is much better to do it properly from the start than to have the water slowly trickling down your neck. Some walkers carry a light cape, but this is useless in a wind and I personally have never bothered with it. I have never known any one to catch cold through getting wet on a mountain ; you may get soaked to the skin and then have a long journey home in an open car, but it won't do you any harm, however much you may shiver and chatter. I cannot explain it, but there it is ; I suppose it is the fresh air and healthy exercise and the absence of germs.

Last, but not least, there is the compass. Half-a-crown is enough to spend on this. An expensive prismatic compass is heavy and un-necessarily elaborate for our purpose. You do not need even the degrees, but just the eight points— N., S., E., and W. ; N.E., S.E., S.W., and N.W.

You must remember that the compass needle points to the magnetic north and not to the true north. The magnetic north varies from year to year, but at present, for the British Isles, it is about 13 degrees to the west of the true north. So make sure that your compass has an arrow, between N. and N.W., marking the magnetic north. On account of the annual variation this will not be absolutely accurate, but it will be quite near enough.

The use of the compass is very simple. Turn it round until the north end of the needle (often coloured blue) is over the arrow marking the magnetic north. It is now set. If you stand on the side of the compass marked E. and look across to W., you are looking westwards, and so on for any direction you like.

The best way to help you to learn the use of the compass is to let you take an imaginary trip over some wild mountain country. If you can make the expedition in reality, so much the better, of course. The Berwyns, in North Wales, will be ideal for our purpose, because they are wild and lonely and you have to depend almost entirely on the compass when the clouds are down.

You will see a map of the district opposite. Our starting-point is Llandrillo, in the Valley of the Dee, between Corwen and Bala. We aim to ascend Cader Fronwen, walk along the ridge to Moel Sych, and then return to our starting-point.

It is warm and trying to drizzle when we reach Llandrillo, and the clouds are lying low on the mountains. You see from the map that there is a convenient lane leading in the direction of Cader Fronwen. The start of this is quite easily found, for it strikes the main road just to the east of the stream which runs through the village. It is hot work at first, but you soon rise above the valley and into more open country. The lane becomes a grassy track and has rough stone walls now in place of hedges. After about twenty or thirty minutes the walls come to an end and you pass through a couple of gates and are on the open moorland. The gates are put there to stop sheep from straying and you must always remember to close them after you. Farmers are usually very decent in allowing people to cross their land, and it is up to ramblers and climbers not to make themselves unpopular.

If you are already hungry there is a perfect spot for a halt down by the stream on the right. The water is cool and fresh and bubbles delightfully through a little green gorge.

The top of the lane is marked on the map, so you know exactly where you are. The height is given also—1,251 feet above sea-level. You are almost into the cloud now ; you can see nothing in front but bare slopes of grass and bracken disappearing into the heavy grey mist. Now, how are you to find the direction of Cader Fronwen ? First set the compass, with the needle over the arrow marking the magnetic north. Then place the map on the ground, so that the top of it is to the north. You can do this more easily if you rest the compass on the map. Now place some straight object (such as a pencil) on the map, so that one edge connects the 1,251 mark, your present position, with the summit of Cader Fronwen. Look along the pencil from the 1,251 end and you are looking straight at Cader Fronwen, though you cannot see it because of the cloud.

However, you do not need to keep your eyes glued to the compass ; in fact for this portion of the journey you can do without it altogether. Just follow the stream up into the cloud, for a mile, or for two miles up to its source ; it does not matter which. If you strike left anywhere between these points and keep going uphill you are bound to reach the summit, where you will find a large cairn of stones. The ascent will probably have taken two or three hours from Llandrillo. If you have got very hot on the way up you have possibly been going too fast. The mountaineer's pace is a slow and steady one—not more than three miles an hour at the most. But the chilly wind at the top will soon cool you down, and after ten minutes' rest you will probably feel like putting on an extra sweater.

Now the real route-finding starts. You will see from the map that you have to strike roughly due south to reach Bwlch Maen Gwynedd, the lowest point on the ridge. ("Bwlch" is the Welsh for what is known in mountaineering circles as a "col"; that is, the lowest point between two peaks.)

There is no definite ridge here, just a rounded heather slope; so the compass is your only guide. There is no need to be too accurate; you have to cross patches of boggy peat and it is hard to keep an absolutely straight line. Once you have got your direction you can put the map in your pocket and just follow the south end of the compass needle.

A mountain mist is never so thick that you cannot see ten or twenty yards in front in the daytime; it isn't like a town fog. You go on down for some time and then find to your dismay that the ground slopes up to your left, although you are still walking due south. You know you should be on a ridge, yet here you are on a slope that rises

43

up to the east. It begins to dawn on you that you don't know where you are and you feel a hopeless baffled sensation. But there is no need to worry ; a little thought is all that is necessary. It is obvious that if the ground slopes up to the left, then the crest of the ridge must be on the left. You have borne a little too far to the right, that is all. So now you must bear a little to the east (left) of south, crossing the slope in a slightly upward direction, and you cannot fail to strike the ridge. You will know you are on the ridge when the ground once more slopes from the north down to the south. Similarly, if you had found that the slope went up on your right, you would have had to bear a little to the west of south.

Once you reach the bwlch all you have to do is to keep going uphill in a southerly direction and you will soon find yourself on the narrower part of the ridge, where no mistake is possible. There is a broken jagged cliff on the left, which looks very deep and mysterious in the swirling cloud, while on the right are gentle grassy slopes. The ridge is quite narrow but not rocky, and it is a very pleasant and breezy walk to the summit of Cader Berwyn (2,712 feet), where there is a nasty eyesore in the shape of a concrete post erected by surveyors.

Now you want to reach Moel Sych, which lies about south-west. Descend in this direction, but pay more attention to keeping on the ridge until it begins to rise again, when all you have to do is to continue going uphill until you arrive at the summit cairn.

Finding the way down is very simple. As you can see from the map, if you take any direction between north and west you will strike one of the streams running down to Llandrillo. The pleasantest and quickest route is to work back to the top of the lane up which you started, but it does not matter if you miss this, since you can be certain of getting back to Llandrillo by following any stream in a downward direction.

You will have realized by now that you find your way mainly by the features of the country, merely using the compass as a rough guide. Even if you were to get completely lost on this Berwyn trip, you could always reach the desired valley by keeping going in a westerly direction.

All this may seem rather like a geography lesson, but it is worth while following it carefully on the map, so that you won't be one of those who are afraid to go up a mountain when there is a mist on top.

Try to get as much practice as possible in compass work. Then, as soon as you can manage it, you should visit some of the Snowdon mountains, where you will have rock scrambling mixed up with the walking. You could have done this at the beginning, but it is much better that you should have gained some knowledge beforehand.

Now the real fun is beginning. Start off on something like the North Ridge of Tryfan. You can first watch the many parties climbing on the Milestone Buttress, which is close to the main road and is so popular that quite frequently there are serious traffic jams. When a rope travelling south meets a rope travelling west the result is apt to be rather like a maypole dance.

The first part of your route is up stones and heather, but at about 2,000 feet you come to the rocks. These are delightful, whitened with nail-marks, covered with holds and very easy, but still—solid rock. No grass ; no soil ; you are climbing on the core of the mountain itself. It would be dangerous to fall here, you feel ; not that there is any risk of your falling, but it is good to feel that your safety depends entirely on your own powers.

Up over the top of Tryfan and across the spiky pinnacles of the Bristly Ridge you feel that it is all a wonderful dream, and yet the rocks under your fingers are so very rough and hard and real, and you feel so energetically alive, that you almost decide that your ordinary life is a dream.

If you are wise you will spend a few days wandering over the neighbouring mountains before you try any serious climbing. The " Horseshoe of Snowdon," starting off with the narrow edge of Crib Goch, the Glyders, the Carnedds—there is unlimited scope. But you must find out the easy ways from guide-books, or from some one who knows, and just use the compass to keep to these ways. For instance, Capel Curig is roughly east of

Tryfan, but if you blithely set off due east from the summit you will soon find yourself on one of the awkward rock-climbs of the East Face.

There are a few tips that may be useful. Sometimes, for no apparent reason, you may suddenly feel weak and limp. This usually means that you are in need of food. You may not notice that you are hungry until you actually begin to eat, but you will observe a great difference afterwards. It is quite a usual thing to mistake hunger for fatigue. Therefore eat little and often. Don't bother about your ordinary meal-times, of course; it is most annoying for the second man, hanging miserably half-way up a vertical pitch, if his leader suddenly looks at his watch, cries " Good Heavens ! One o'clock ! Lunch-time ! " and lets go of the rope to get out his sandwiches.

If you do get really tired you will find it a great help to eat a little sugar or chocolate every few minutes. Actually you will discover that you can keep going a long time after you think yourself exhausted.

Always keep up a slow and steady pace, with few rests. You will find this method quicker in the long run, and much less tiring than rushing at top speed and having to rest every few minutes.

Last but not least, don't leave litter about. Bury all scraps under stones, or else take them back with you in the rucksack. You should leave no signs at all that you have been there. You may think that your little bit of rubbish won't make much difference to the vast mountains, but the sight of one paper bag takes away a lot of the pleasure, and besides, if all the thousands of people who ever visit the mountains were to leave all their paper and orange peel behind, then the whole district would be one great rubbish heap. It is part of the code of the climber to be very particular on this point.

Chapter IV

THE ROCK-CLIMB

YOU are on your way to do a real rock-climb ;
and not only that, but a climb that is classified
as " Very Difficult " into the bargain. A kindly
climber has taken pity on your eagerness and offered
to take you out with him.

There are six standards of difficulty—Easy,
Moderate, Difficult, Very Difficult, Severe, and
Very Severe. You realize that the forthcoming
ascent is going to be quite a test for you.

We will call the route the Nameless Buttress.
It is ideal for your purpose, because it includes
examples of almost every kind of problem that you
are likely to meet. In fact, it is too good to be true.

You are half-way up the final scree-slope below
the cliff itself. The other two are several hundred
feet below, strolling up lazily. One is puffing at a
curly pipe and you can see the smoke against the
deep blue of the little tarn so far below. You are
too thrilled to linger and have excitedly rushed on
ahead. You have borrowed a pair of climbing-boots
and put on your oldest clothes and feel that, at any
rate, you look like a climber.

You are almost at the foot of the rocks now.

They do not look so steep now that you are directly below, and you notice that they are quite broken-up after all. From a distance the precipice had looked as sheer as the side of a house.

Your companions join you almost before you have finished puffing, and you all move over to a little cairn at the bottom of a massive buttress that juts out a good deal in front of the rest of the cliff. You rope up here, using two 80-foot ropes. You are tied on in the middle, so that you have two ropes round your waist. The leader starts off and soon reaches a stance. Then he pulls in the rope until it is nearly taut, and up you go. The rocks are grey and very rough. They are quite dry, but you notice that some of the crevices look a little damp and muddy.

This pitch is just simple scrambling, and you rejoin your leader without any trouble. The stance is a comfortable little grass ledge, and as soon as you arrive the leader takes off his belay and shows you how to belay yourself. There is a convenient spike of rock just above. You pass the rope round this and pull it, until the rope between you and the belay is tight when you are standing on the ledge. Now, as close to the belay as possible, take hold of the rope that runs down to the third man and pass a small loop of it under your waist-line. Now there are two equal lengths of rope running from the belay to you. Tie your loop in a single knot round the two lengths of rope between you and the belay, and you are firmly secured to the mountain.

A reference to the photograph opposite page 29 will help you to understand this better.

You will see now that, whatever happens, you cannot be pulled off. You will also have a ready answer to the question so often asked by non-climbers : " What is the use of the rope, anyhow ? If one man falls don't all the others get pulled off ? " Or if you get too irritated by a stupid questioner you can always reply, " Yes ! We just have the rope to make it more dangerous."

This method of belaying is used for all members of the party, leader and followers. Well, now you have to bring up No. 3. You must not try to hold him with your hands alone. First pull in the rope until it is taut. Then put it under one arm, say the left arm, behind the back and over the right shoulder, so that it hangs down in front of your chest, where you hold it with the right hand. The portion of the rope going down to No. 3 should be under the left armpit. The right hand is used for holding and the left hand is used just for feeling your man, unless he comes off, of course, in which case both hands come into play. Owing to the friction of the rope over your back there is no difficulty at all in holding a man's weight. And if you have tied yourself closely to the belay you cannot be pulled even a few inches.

Keep the rope almost taut, but don't pull. Take it in evenly as No. 3 ascends, so that there will be no jerking and no slack rope.

No. 3 does not need to belay, but he can if

he wishes for safety's sake, though he has no holding to do. Now the leader goes on. You keep on your belay and hold the rope as before, except that it goes up from under your arm, instead of down as before. This is your most important job. Your function now is to see that the rope runs smoothly ; the slightest jerk might easily pull the leader off a delicate section. You must also be prepared to hold him if he should fall. There is a terrific strain, of course, if a man falls from above, and that is why careful belaying is so much more important when you are seconding the leader than when you are merely bringing up the man below. You cannot do much in the case of a big drop, but you must be prepared to do all you can. Under no circumstances must you take off your belay until your leader has reached a safe stance. You must not keep the rope taut between yourself and the leader ; leave a couple of feet of slack in case he makes a sudden move.

The next pitch is a slab. It is smooth but does not look very difficult, since the angle is quite gentle. However, holds polished white tell of many scraping boot-nails. The leader mounts neatly and quickly, and you do not bother to watch him very closely. It all looks so simple. Then your turn comes. Now that you come to examine it, the first foothold looks much too small to hold your big boots. It is only 2 feet off the ground. You step carefully on to it and, much to your surprise, your foot does not slip. The next foothold is

A WALL.

A strenuous practice climb, on sandstone, at Helsby, Cheshire.

A SLAB (IVY CHIMNEY ROUTE,
MILESTONE BUTTRESS).

The climber is standing correctly, well
away from the rock. The left knee is a little
too close to the slab.

smaller still. With a great effort you manage to reach a little fingerhold, but now you are lying flat against the slab. Still in this position, you put your boot in the next foothold ; it slips off ; you hang for a moment on two fingers and then slide gently back to the ledge. You begin to feel rather annoyed and the following conversation ensues :

You (*slightly peeved*). Why did my foot slip off that hold ? Yours stayed on all right. It must be my boots.

LEADER (*irritatingly calm*). Just think a moment. How would you set about it if you wanted to slide down a slope ?

You. Just lie on my back and slide, I suppose.

LEADER. Well, isn't that exactly what you were doing, except that you were lying on your tummy instead of your back ? When you're going upstairs you don't lie against the steps and pull yourself up by the stair-rods. Not unless you're drunk, anyhow. You just walk up in an upright position. Now try again.

You step up once more and then put your right foot again on the small second hold. Standing straight upright, away from the rock, you find you cannot reach the high fingerhold. However there is a little pocket lower down and this is quite enough to enable you to keep your balance. You step up on to the small foothold, raising yourself by the strength of your legs instead of trying to pull yourself up, against the friction of the rough rock, by the much inferior strength of your arms. You find

53

that you can stand quite comfortably and can now reach better holds which lead you easily to the top of the pitch. You have now learnt a valuable lesson—to keep your body away from the rock, climb on your feet and use your hands to keep your balance. Your legs are obviously stronger than your arms ; if you don't believe this try to do a twenty-mile walk on your hands.

The stance is too small for three people, so the leader has to proceed before the third man can come up. You must now pay all your attention to the leader until he is safely belayed on the next stance. Then you may bring up No. 3. The next pitch is a wall ; that is, a face of rock that is vertical or nearly so. Here you must take a fair portion of your weight on your hands, but you can greatly ease the arm-strain by pushing up with your feet. You decide first what holds you are going to use and then ascend fairly quickly, so as not to get tired. You are learning the value of thinking calmly about each move without getting flurried, and half-way up you pause on a good foothold to consider the next few steps. Your leader encourages you by telling you that you have made a very neat job of the pitch.

The rocks above overhang threateningly, but they are split by a chimney, a dark three-sided cleft some 3 feet in width. Here you use a thread-belay, passing a loop of your rope through a muddy hole behind a chockstone jammed in the chimney and tying it round the stone or on to your waist-line.

Thus you are firmly secured to the chockstone. You must make sure that the chockstone is reliable, of course, before doing this. It is often an awkward job threading the rope and then fishing about in the recesses of the crack to pull the end through, and a lot of time and trouble can be saved by carrying about with you a 4-foot spare length of rope or line. This is tied in a loop round the chockstone and each member of the party can tie on to it in turn.

The best holds are on the left-hand side of the chimney, so you put your feet against this left wall and your back against the right wall. It looks very forbidding and impossible, and you don't quite see how you can get up without more holds. However you put your left foot up a little, then push your back up, with the palms of your hands below you against the wall behind, and very soon you find you are quite a good way up. This is known as backing-up. It makes you hot and tired, but now and again you arrive at a good foothold, where you can rest in perfect security, wedged across the cleft. Actually, even without any holds at all, it is possible to hold the full weight of a man below when you are thus braced across a chimney.

You are about 20 feet up now and you notice that there are good holds on the right as well as on the left wall. You now keep only your left foot on the left wall, push out from the right wall with your right hand, place the right foot on one of the holds on the right wall and with your left hand grasp a handhold on the left wall. This all sounds very complicated, but is is actually quite simple when you come to do it. You are now standing astride the chimney, looking inwards, with the left hand and foot on the left wall and the right hand and foot on the right wall. You can now climb straight up in this more natural position. This is known as bridging and is less tiring than backing-up.

At intervals you find chockstones jammed at the back of the chimney and some of these will be of great assistance. But don't make a dive into the recesses of the chimney just because you feel safer there; you will probably find it much more strenuous.

You arrive at the top triumphant, but rather tired and perhaps a little bruised.

The rocks above look impossible, but there is a tempting-looking ledge, at your level, about 20 feet to the right. To reach this a traverse is necessary. You see the leader safely across this and then bring up the third man. You now realize why you have been allotted the middle position on the rope; you can be held from both sides whilst making the horizontal traverse.

You have to cross a steep wall that drops giddily down beneath you for over 100 feet. It is an alarming feeling, stepping off from a good ledge into space, as it were. However, you take the plunge and step carefully out on to a small foothold. You focus on your feet and find that you don't notice the height. The holds are small but good,

56

and you find you can often make progress by pulling yourself forward on a vertical rib. It is quite a relief to be moving sideways instead of having the effort of climbing up. Balance is everything here. It is really only walking on small holds, using your hands to keep your balance.

At the end of the traverse there is a holdless section of about 5 feet. With a great effort you manage to reach the stance with your right foot, with the result that you are spread-eagled against the rock. It is aggravating to have one foot on your goal and be unable to get the rest of your body over. But there are no handholds at all. Then the leader points out a thin vertical crack at the near end of the stance, and by pulling sideways on the edge of this with your right hand you are able to gain the roomy comfort of the ledge.

The next pitch is a nasty-looking vertical crack. It seems to have no holds at all except for two small chockstones about 20 feet up, and the rock on either side, though rough, is also holdless. You watch the leader carefully—he makes it look quite easy—and then try to imitate him when your turn comes.

You bury one arm up to the elbow in the crack and then jam your right boot as high up as possible. With a heave you pull up, jam the left boot a little above the right and bury the other arm. This goes on for about 15 feet and then the crack gets narrower. You are still able to make your boots stay in by turning the toes sideways, but the hands are the difficulty. You insert one hand and close the fist, which now forms a kind of human chockstone. Pulling bodily on this you are able to grasp one of the real chockstones and your difficulties are over.

Your fingers are by now so tired that you can hardly hang on, but luckily the top portion of the crack is wide enough to accommodate a leg and a shoulder, and you manage to struggle rather clumsily to a wide, restful grass ledge. You sprawl down, shaky but pleased.

There is ample room for the third man and when he arrives the leader suggests a rest. He does not look as though he needed it, but you are very thankful. Some chocolate is eaten and then out come the pipes. No. 3 points pityingly to a party of ramblers working slowly up the grassy slopes above the lake. "Poor devils! They must be hot slogging up that slope on a day like this. It just about creased me getting up to the cliff."

You say nothing. You do not envy the walkers, but privately you decide that they are having a much easier time of it. You feel very superior, however.

The party begins to show some signs of life. "This is the crux of the climb," says the leader pleasantly, "a layback."

You look up, wondering what on earth a layback is. You are soon to know.

The crack ahead is only 12 or 15 feet high, but it overhangs all the way and seems to have no holds. A great flake of rock is separated from the main mass by this narrow crack, like a door that is opened so wide that the handle almost touches the wall. The leader grasps the vertical edge of the flake at shoulder-level, places his right foot against the main rock at almost the same height, puts the other foot beside it and begins to work up. He is bent double, with the soles of his boots pressed flat against the rock only a few inches away from his hands, which are pulling at the sharp opposite edge of the crack. The harder he pulls with his arms the harder will his feet be pressed against the rock and therefore the less likely to slip. The strain on the arms is terrific. He must keep moving, so that he will reach the top before he becomes exhausted. You feel thankful that there is a nice large grass ledge just below him.

The leader moves first one foot and then one hand. If he gets his hands much above his feet it is less strain on his arms, but then his feet begin to slip. This goes on for about 8 feet before he is able to grab a hidden handhold and haul himself, panting, on to the ledge at the top.

You are secretly pleased to know that it is possible for an expert to show signs of fatigue, but rather dubious about your own chances. Now your turn comes. You manage to get your hands and your feet up, close together in the approved style, but then it is as much as you can do even to hang on for a few seconds, let alone attempt to climb up. No. 3 sees that your fingers are tired and kindly offers you a shoulder, letting you stand on his back without a murmur, then slowly straightening and raising you up. Even now that you can reach a good handhold you have a great struggle to finish the pitch. Your pride is somewhat restored when the third man asks for " a slight pull."

The next pitch is a groove—a shallow depression with a muddy crack at the back—and this is much easier. You climb it partly by bridging and partly by using holds in the crack.

There is another wall ahead, but it is rather different from the previous one. Half-way up is a ledge, about 2 feet wide, with no holds for some distance above. You pull up on the edge of this ledge and then make a sort of spring, getting your chest and shoulders above your hands and half-way over the ledge. You are now pushing up on your hands and you struggle until you can get one knee on the ledge. Now, balancing carefully on one hand, you slowly raise the other to a small hold, just within reach, and get your feet on to the ledge. This is known as a mantelshelf, and you can obtain excellent practice for this type of problem on any ordinary mantelpiece at home.

"And now for the hand-traverse," says the leader cheerfully. You wish he wouldn't be so beastly hearty about it.

You climb up for a few feet and look at the traverse. It is an almost horizontal leaf of rock, running out to the left under an overhang. The longer you look at it the less you like it, so you decide that the sooner you start the better. You grasp the sharp edge, let your legs hang uselessly below and swing along on your hands. A little way along the rock becomes less steep, and you draw your knees up against the slab to take some of the strain off your arms. You are at the end of the traverse now and have only to pull up to a hold a couple of feet higher to achieve victory ; but you have no strength left in your arms. A slight pull by the leader makes all the difference and you are up.

Only one more pitch now—an arête. This is a sharp exposed edge, not quite vertical, but fairly steep. It is like the apex of a house-roof, only tilted up at a high angle.

You really enjoy this pitch. The situation is thrillingly airy, yet the rock is perfect—firm and rough—and the holds are thoroughly satisfying. You look appreciatively down the sheer drop of 300 feet and think how wonderful it is that you can feel so safe. Even without the safeguard of the rope above you would not be nervous ; in fact you have almost forgotten that it is there.

You are at the top at last, filled with a feeling of indescribable satisfaction. All the mountains and precipices look different ; you are viewing them now with the eyes of a rock-climber. You feel a kind of pity for the non-climber, who can never have the chance of enjoying such sensations. You have earned your rest and can now relax and lie back in glorious idleness.

You feel pleasantly tired and a little weak about

the wrists and shoulders. Your companions appear to be quite fresh, although they do not look very muscular fellows ; in fact the leader is of rather a slight build. You realize that you must have wasted a great deal of energy by not doing things the right way.

A climb such as you have just done would be described in a climbers' guide-book as follows :—

THE NAMELESS BUTTRESS

350 feet. An interesting and varied climb, strenuous in parts. Pitches short and safe. Some fine situations. Rock perfect throughout.

Standard.—Very difficult. Pitch 7 Severe.

Rope.—70 feet.

Start.—Begin at the lowest point of the cliff, at the foot of the most prominent buttress. (Cairn.) The route follows a fairly straight line up the middle of the broad lower part of the buttress and then keeps as nearly as possible on the crest of the narrow upper half.

(1) 30 feet. Easy scrambling to stance and belay.

(2) 35 feet. An amusing and rather delicate slab leads to a small stance.

(3) 25 feet. A steep wall is climbed on good holds. (Thread belay.)

(4) 40 feet. The strenuous chimney above the belay is climbed by backing-up and bridging.

(5) 30 feet. A delicate traverse to the right, with an awkward step at the end, leads to a small ledge in an exposed situation.

(6) 30 feet. A strenuous crack is climbed to a broad ledge.

(7) 12 feet. A large flake rests against the wall. The crack behind this is climbed by a layback, very exhausting to start. The situation is perfectly safe.

(8) 60 feet. Climb the pleasant but slightly greasy groove immediately ahead.

(9) 20 feet. A rather tricky mantelshelf problem.

(10) 20 feet. Ascend for 10 feet and then make a 10-foot hand-traverse along the obvious edge to the left. The pull-up at the end is trying for tired arms.

(11) 50 feet. An exposed arête, well provided with good holds, provides a delightful finish to the climb.

You will notice that the guide divides the route into pitches. Although often not mentioned, you can take it that there is a belay at the top of each pitch. You will notice also that the guide tells you merely how to find the climb ; it does not tell you how to do it. That is left for you to work out for yourself. It needs a lot of imagination to visualize, from the bare guide-book description, all the thrills and excitements of the ascent.

Chapter V

EQUIPMENT AND PRACTICE AT HOME

YOU may not actually have done a real rock-climb, but at any rate you are now familiar with all the climbing terms from your imaginary ascent of the Nameless Buttress. Mantelshelves are no longer connected with anything so commonplace as fireplaces ; walls are no longer made of bricks and mortar ; chimneys do not smoke, however heated the language that issues from their depths.

You have also got a theoretical idea as to how you must tackle every type of problem. You will now be itching to get on with the real thing. How, then, can you make a start ?

To begin with, you must have the necessary equipment. We will deal first with clothing. Nothing very special is needed for summer climbing ; if you follow the lines set out in the chapter on mountain walking you won't go far wrong. Grey flannels, tucked inside the stockings below the knees, are very comfortable ; they also give one the appearance of having enormous calf muscles, like the dandies of old who used to pad their silken hose for this reason. Plus-fours are popular, though unnecessarily baggy, and breeches are probably as good as anything if they are not too tight. Riding-breeches usually suffer in this respect. Whatever you may choose you must be able to lift the knee as high with them as without them.

Special climbing-jackets are made, after the style of golf-jackets. You should, if possible, get one of windproof material—closely-woven cotton—but this is entirely wasted unless it fits closely at the neck, cuffs, and waist. However, an old sports jacket will do very well, but see that it allows you to raise your arms freely above your head or else they will very soon get tired. Also, carry a safety-pin, so that you can fasten up the collar.

You must remember that climbing is a much colder business than walking, since you are standing still at least half of the time. This is not merely a matter of comfort. If you are not wearing enough clothes the first parts to suffer will be the fingers, and you cannot climb safely if you have lost all feeling in your fingers. Therefore carry a couple of spare sweaters if it seems at all likely to be cold ; you need not put them on until you reach the foot of your climb.

On a hot day climb in shorts by all means. It will do your style a world of good. You will think twice about using your bare knees on a jagged hold. You will discover that neatness makes a lot of difference even in a chimney. And if you return with your knees a bleeding mass, you will hide them in shame ; for they are not honourable scars of battle, but merely evidence of clumsy climbing.

You may wish to know why it is considered bad style to use your knees. Try getting on to a table on your knees alone and then see how high you can reach. You will find that you have gained very little height. Now come down and step on to the table, with the help of your hands if necessary, and you will probably be able to reach the ceiling. You have far more scope for reaching high holds when you are standing on your feet, and also you are better in balance. I have seen too many climbers with both knees on a narrow ledge and their legs sticking out horizontally behind, unable to move either up or down. I have done it myself, so I know what it feels like. There are many occasions, of course, when you have to use your knees ; but use your feet whenever possible.

Now we come to the very important question of boots. Buy as good a pair as you can afford. When I started climbing I could not afford to fork out three or four pounds, so I purchased a pair of strong walking-boots for about a guinea and with great labour nailed them myself. Before the war you could buy quite a decent pair, ready nailed, for twenty-five shillings or so.

Climbing-boots should not come much above the ankle-bone. If you get a pair that is too high, be ruthless and cut off the tops. They will then be much more comfortable for walking and much more efficient on small holds. The tongues should be sewn all the way to the top, so that the boots are completely waterproof, and there should be no hooks for the laces, but holes all the way up. There are few things more irritating than hooks that get either bent down or else broken off.

Choose a boot that will fit you comfortably with a couple of thick socks inside. Your toes should just fail to touch the end of the boot, but make sure that when you stand with one toe-nail (of the boot, not of your foot) on a small hold, the front of your boot does not curl up and look at you.

There is no need for climbing-boots to be very heavy and clumsy ; four pounds the pair is quite a satisfactory weight. But see that the sole is stiff ; it is most difficult to keep a nail on a small hold if the sole is bending up.

The tag at the back should be of leather, one-piece with the boot, and it is a good feature if the back of the boot is protected by a wide piece of leather instead of the narrow strip usually fitted. This makes the stitching less likely to go, and also makes it a less serious matter if it does go.

Leather laces are quite satisfactory, but personally I prefer cord ; they last longer and do not so easily come undone.

The question of nailing is largely a matter of personal taste. The old-fashioned clinkers are still very popular. These are iron nails, with roughly oblong heads which are set at right-angles to the edge of the sole. They have long shanks, which are driven right through the sole, so that they come out outside the upper. The head of the nail has a protecting flange over the edge of the sole, and the end of the shank is bent over to meet this, thus forming a complete ring of metal.

It is a skilled job nailing with clinkers, since no holes should be made beforehand. If properly inserted, however, they stay in well. If one does come out, though, it is liable to take with it a chunk of leather. Clinkers can be used only round the edge of the sole and heel—here the shanks go right in and are not bent over—of course, and for the middle of the sole something of the nature of ordinary hobnails will have to be used.

The other common outside nail is the tricouni. This is made of hard steel and has three prongs, and it has also two barbed prongs which are driven into the sole of the boot. It is kept flat on the sole by a small plate of soft iron, which has holes for two small ordinary nails to give additional firmness. This is known as the No. 1 tricouni.

There are various newer types of tricounis, of which perhaps the best is the No. 6. This has not such a narrow gripping edge as the No. 1, and therefore I do not favour it for the sides of the boot, but it is quite useful for the toes since it is not likely to be snapped off by a sudden kick against a rock. It is fixed in by staples, and its main disadvantage is that these staples are liable to come loose and need hammering in again.

For the inner part of the sole muggers, rough wrought iron hobnails, are excellent, though No. 1 tricounis can also be used in this position.

STANDARD ALPINE
CLINKER.

Weight 2½ oz. per doz.
Price 1/- per doz.

MUGGERS.

Large, Weight 1¼ oz.
per doz.
Small, Weight 1 oz.
per doz.
Price 3d. per doz.

No. 6 TRICOUNI.

Weight 6 oz. per doz.
Price 4/- per doz.

No. 1 TRICOUNI

Weight 2¼ oz. per doz.
Price 2/- per doz.

Reproduced by courtesy of Robert Lawrie Limited, 38 Bryanston St., London, W.1.

NAILS FOR CLIMBING-BOOTS.

Now for the theory of nails. Clinkers and muggers, being made of soft iron, give a friction grip ; that is to say the hard rock bites into the soft iron. Tricounis, on the other hand, give a lock-hold ; they catch in some little crevice and stay there, which is obviously more scientific, and for that reason I prefer them for serious rock-climbing. You can choose the tiniest hold, fit one nail in it and know that you are safe.

Therefore I recommend No. 1 tricounis round the edge of the sole, with perhaps No. 6's or clinkers in the toe. Now it is useful to have some friction grip for chimneys, so muggers may be put in the middle. Clinkers are best in the heel, which has not much delicate work to do, with perhaps a couple of muggers in the middle. The boots in the group opposite page 79 are nailed in this way, which will help to give you some idea of the spacing of the nails.

If you want to concentrate more on walking and do not intend to do any difficult climbing, I should recommend clinkers all round the sole. At the same time it must be admitted that many expert climbers swear by clinkers for rock-work. You usually find, however, that these clinker-fiends have abnormally strong arms, and therefore do not have to rely so much on their feet as do weaker mortals.

The very most important item of all your equipment is the rope. You must buy one of the few brands that have been passed by the Alpine Club. The average climbing-rope is about half an inch in diameter and weighs a little over 5 pounds for 100 feet. It is guaranteed to stand a strain of close on $1\frac{1}{2}$ tons, which is equal to an average-sized man falling about 10 feet. This gives you some idea of the terrific strains that may be involved. However, these tests were taken directly over a beam, while in climbing such a lot of friction is taken up by the rope passing round the second's back and probably running for some distance through his hands, that in actual practice the rope scarcely ever breaks. If it does you may be practically certain that it has cut itself over a rough edge of rock.

If a great strain comes on a rope it stretches enormously. Thus there is no sudden jerk. That is the secret of its strength. An old rope loses its elasticity and consequently may be unsafe, even though it looks perfectly sound. Be very careful to keep your rope away from any acid, which will make it as weak as cotton without leaving any visible sign that anything is wrong. Do not store it in too dry a place or it may become brittle. A wash-house or anywhere not too damp or actually exposed to the weather will do.

A big shock weakens a rope. If it has had to withstand a strain anywhere near its breaking-point it will never be safe to use again. A moderate strain—a leader falling a few feet on a sloping slab, for instance—will weaken it temporarily, but it will recover, partially or completely, in a day or two. It will be obvious that climbing-ropes should not be used for purposes such as towing cars.

Inspect your rope now and then to make sure that it has not got cut or frayed. Remember that human lives depend on it—not only your own, but other people's as well. If an accident occurs through the breaking of your faulty rope, then you are morally responsible.

For some reason beginners are always advised to use rope in preference to line. Line is only about half the weight of rope, and there are other things to be said in its favour. It does not get so stiff and kinky when wet and it can be used on much smaller belays. Personally, I always use it. On the other hand, of course, it is only half as strong. Perhaps the best thing you can do is to compromise and buy a three-quarter weight rope.

Whatever weight you choose, get a 100-foot length. You will find it more than you need for most climbs, but that only means a little extra to pull in at the top of each pitch. Many accidents have happened through the leader not having enough rope to reach a belay. Before the war 100 feet cost roughly from 12s. 6d. to a guinea, depending on whether rope or line was bought. For three persons you will need twice as much, of course, though it is not a serious matter if the rope between No. 2 and No. 3 is too short.

Now you will wish to know where you can buy all your equipment. I do not want to mention any names, so I suggest that you look at the advertisements in the journals of any of the well-known climbing clubs, such as the following : Alpine Club, Climbers' Club, Fell and Rock Climbing Club (Lake District), Rucksack Club (Manchester), Scottish Mountaineering Club, and Wayfarers' Club (Liverpool). You can obtain them from many booksellers and also at public libraries.

Now you must learn some more about the management of the rope. Probably the most satisfactory knot for the end man is the double

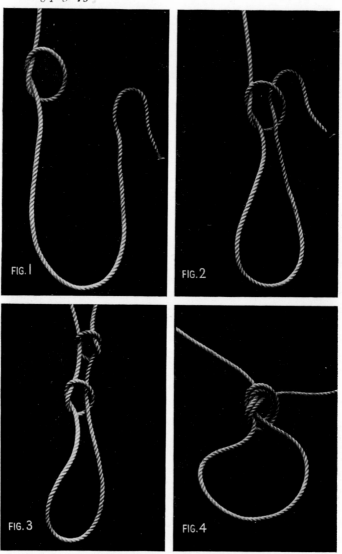

KNOTS.

FIGS. 1, 2, and 3.—Double fisherman's bend, for the end man.
FIG. 4.—Overhand loop, for the middle man.

fisherman's bend. This is quite simple to learn.

First tie a single knot about 4 feet from the end of the rope (see opposite, Fig. 1). Now put the end 4 feet of the rope round your waist and thread the actual end through the knot (Fig. 2), forming a slip-knot. Tighten this up until it fits closely, but not uncomfortably, round the waist.

Unless you are unduly fat there should now be about 12 inches to spare at the end of the rope. Bring this over the main rope, bend it back and under both ropes, bring it up and then thread it down through the loop that is now formed of the spare 12 inches (Fig. 3). You have now two slip-knots, working against each other, and all that remains is to tighten up the outer one against the inner.

When you come to do the actual tying, with the aid of the illustrations, you will find that the whole business is not nearly so complicated as it sounds.

The main advantages of this knot are that it is easy to adjust and easy to untie. It cannot come undone if 3 inches spare are left at the end of the rope.

The bowline is also quite satisfactory, but is not so simple to tie. There is no need for you to learn more than the one end-man's knot.

For the middle-man the ordinary overhand loop is the usual choice. This is extremely simple to make. Double the rope in the middle (or wherever you wish to tie on) and tie a knot in the doubled portion, so that a loop large enough to slip over the shoulders is left (Photo, Fig. 4). This can then be tightened to fit the waist.

Now the next thing to do is to see what practice in climbing problems and, especially, in the use of the rope you can get at home.

Trees are invaluable in this respect. Don't pick on Father's prize fruit tree, or you will make yourself unpopular. Non-climbers are so unreasonable. Choose a good big tree, but make sure that it hasn't a lot of dead branches. These may give very good practice in the use of rotten rock ; but you will look silly sticking feet uppermost out of a cucumber frame.

If you haven't any suitable trees at home and are not near the country, there are always the city parks. You can count the park-keepers as avalanches and keep out of their track. A friend of mine used to practise sleeping-out on these lines. He would slip into a Manchester park at dead of night and settle comfortably down in his sleeping-bag in the bandstand. If he overslept he had to dodge outraged guardians of the law, who were far more terrifying than any ordinary mountaineering hazard.

You learnt all about belaying in the previous chapter, and now you can practise it. Climb up your tree to a good solid branch and belay yourself to a higher branch. You can be either sitting or standing.

Now get a friend, properly roped, to climb up below you. Hold the rope in your hands alone and tell him to jump off when he is a few feet above the ground. You may be able to hold him, but it will be a great strain. Or the rope may run through your hands, with painful results if you don't let go quickly. In any case it will be obvious that you cannot hold a man's weight for long on your hands alone. It is even more obvious that you would have no chance of checking a falling body in this fashion.

Now hold the rope correctly—under one arm and over the other shoulder. In this position you will find that you can hold your companion's weight for as long as you wish. If your shoulder becomes tired it is quite simple to slip the rope down to the waist, even with the weight on it. The strain then comes more directly on the belay and less on you. You are not, however, well placed for giving a pull in this position.

When your victim obediently jumps off into space your feet may be pulled off the bough. This means that you have left some slack between yourself and the belay. However, you are safely secured and cannot go far. You are perfectly safe with a good belay even if there is no stance at all, but a stance without a belay is just a snare and a delusion ; it gives nothing but a false sense of security.

Now you must see what it feels like to pull some one up. Tell your long-suffering friend to hang limply, without helping himself at all. Now try and pull him up. You will feel quite exhausted before you have raised him a yard, and if there is a lot of friction with the rope running over branches you may find it impossible to move him at all.

Next, if any signs of life remain and you are still on speaking terms, ask him to help himself with his feet. This will make your task easier, but you still have practically his whole weight to deal with. However, if he uses his hands, if only for scratching at the bark of the tree, you will find that you can pull him up quite effectively. If the leader has got up a pitch the most inexpert second can always follow somehow, unless he absolutely refuses to help himself. It will work wonders in such a case if you get out your penknife and say sadly, " It's a pity to cut this good rope, but there's nothing else for it."

There is one more important piece of technique for you to learn—" abseiling," or roping-down. This is invaluable if you get stuck and are unable to descend by ordinary methods, besides being very spectacular yet perfectly safe.

Climb up until you are near the top of the tree. To abseil you must be unroped. Hang the rope over a higher bough, so that it hangs down on either side and both ends are resting on the ground. You thus have a double rope to slide down. It will be obvious that for a 50-foot abseil you need a 100-foot rope.

Stand so that the double rope is hanging down in front of you. Place it between your legs, bring it round the back of the left thigh and up to the front of the chest and let it hang over your left elbow, which must be kept sharply bent.

You hold on to the rope above you with both hands. The friction of the rope running round your body is so great that you can easily stop without holding on at all with your hands, provided you keep your elbow bent. In fact, if the rope is wet it is quite difficult to move. Even a dry rope is apt to stick ; line is probably preferable here.

Descend at a steady speed, keeping your feet flat against the tree trunk and walking down, with your body at an angle of about 45 degrees. Take care not to leave your feet behind or you will fall out of everything.

If you want to know what it feels like to abseil an overhang, you can descend well away from the trunk. You will spin round at first, but not for long.

Lower down you will notice that you slide more easily. That is because there is less weight of rope below and therefore less friction over the elbow.

There are various other methods of abseiling. Many climbers prefer to let the rope run over the shoulder, in preference to the bent elbow. The weakness of this procedure is that the rope may slip off.

Then again, there are elaborate " safety " schemes, whereby a complicated rope-cradle is made. These are extremely safe, since the climber is usually unable to move an inch. He hangs there, like a trussed chicken, until he has exhausted himself by his frantic efforts. Then he has a rest and decides that it would be easier to climb down after all.

I have seen a couple of hours wasted in this way on a single abseil in the Alps. Yet with half an hour's previous practice you can be sure of wasting no time on the rocks.

When you reach the ground all you have to do is to pull on one end of the rope—a single thickness this time, not the doubled rope—and the other end will be pulled up until it drops off the bough. Actually, on rocks the rope is often inclined to catch behind the belay and it usually pays to have it threaded through a spare loop, which has to be left behind, of course.

Once you have learnt to do an abseil you can be perfectly sure of being able to descend in safety from any difficulty, provided that you are able to gain a belay and that your rope is long enough to reach from belay to belay below you.

In the Alps a great deal of abseiling is done to save time and energy, often in places that could be descended by ordinary climbing. But it does not save either time or energy if you take an hour over a single pitch. So go on practising until you feel thoroughly confident about the whole thing.

Notice the difference when you try sliding down the rope, from a lower branch, in the ordinary gymnasium manner. You will find a climbing-rope too thin to grasp with your feet, and consequently all the strain will come on your arms. Before I had learnt to abseil I descended a 40-foot pitch on

EQUIPMENT.

Rope (120-foot Alpine line), boots, rubbers, crampons, Alpine goggles, lantern, ice-axes.

The boots are nailed with No. 6 tricounis in the toes, No. 1 tricounis round the soles, muggers in the middle, and clinkers round the heels. The boot on the right has crampons (rather short) attached.

Note the ice-axe sling. The " stop-screw " can just be seen near the bottom of the axe.

Note also the leather cover on the left-hand axe, a great convenience in travelling.

a small sandstone cliff at Helsby, in Cheshire. I used only a single thickness of line and took a turn round my right wrist to provide additional support. All went well—or fairly well—until I reached the overhang, 15 feet from the bottom. Then I lost control, and the line ran round my wrist and burnt it almost to the bone.

There were some small boys at the bottom, watching with great interest, as well they might. I had to pretend, of course, that I had meant to come down in that fashion, and took my tingling and unwilling hands hurriedly up another climb.

While you are still on the tree you may as well get the feel of climbing up the rope. You will find that with your feet against the trunk you can do this for some distance.

There are other bits of climbing technique you can practise at home. With a door wide open you will be able to back-up the opening. It will be unfortunate, though, if somebody slams the door when you are half-way up.

Then you can practise a hand-traverse along the top of a wall or a strong gutter. It is very useful to know just how far you can go on your hands alone.

A rough stone wall sometimes gives good practice in the use of small holds, especially if you are able to make a traverse along a good length of it.

You can put in some good work on an old-fashioned mantelpiece. It is easy enough to raise yourself on to your hands, but surprisingly awkward actually to obtain a footing ; a very delicate balance is needed. It is a good plan first to crowd the mantelpiece with all the ornaments that you most detest—those china dogs presented by Uncle Joe can take a front place. A slight slip on your part— most unfortunate accident—and they are no more.

If you have a slate roof—say of an outhouse— not too far from the ground, you can learn the theory of slab-climbing. You will find that you can walk on it, with care, in climbing-boots. The slates won't suffer much if you are careful, and anyhow it is all in a good cause.

Now imagine you are reaching up for a high handhold and lean inwards until you are almost against the slates. Your feet will slip, and you will probably slide down to the gutter. This should convince you that you must stand straight upright on slabs and not lean in at all. The lesson will be made even more convincing if you miss the gutter and break your neck in the yard below.

CHAPTER VI

LEADING

NOW you are ready to start climbing in earnest. You feel, probably, that you have done quite enough book-work and playing about on trees, and now you are ready for some more serious work. If you have had a few days of walking and scrambling and can find your way in a mist, and if you feel quite happy and confident on scrambles like Crib Goch and the Bristly Ridge, and if you have practised the " exercises " in the last chapter, then you are far better equipped than I was when I started on the rocks.

It will be all to the good if you can get an experienced man to take you up a few climbs. But start leading as soon as possible. If you once get into the habit of following you will never have the confidence to lead. There are many climbers who can follow neatly up the most difficult routes and yet are afraid to lead the simplest little pitches. So when you are second or third on the rope try and forget that you are held from above. Make every move as carefully as though your life depended on it.

Possibly you may have no one to start you off.

That need not worry you at all; in many ways it is all to the good. You will learn to depend on yourself from the very beginning. There is much more merit in leading an easy climb than in following up a difficult one; a good leader can get the clumsiest novice up most routes.

If you select suitable climbs, two or three of you can start off together with perfect safety, even without any previous experience. All should do a certain amount of leading, but if one is keener and obviously better than the others he will probably step naturally into first place on the rope.

How and where can you start? I will deal first with North Wales, since I know that best of all.

You must buy an Ordnance Survey 1-inch-to-mile map of the district and the series of guide-books issued by the Climbers' Club. Nearly all the good Welsh climbing is in the Snowdon district, and your most convenient centre is probably the Ogwen Valley, between Capel Curig and Bangor. You can stay at a farmhouse or hotel, or else you can camp.

A splendid initial climb is Little Tryfan. You can make the first pitch easy by keeping to the right, or hard by tackling it on the left, and then you gain a delightful 200-foot arête, just like the apex of a roof tilted at about 45 degrees. It is mainly slab-work—quite exposed, but easy if you remember to stand upright on your holds—and the rock is perfect. It is an excellent place for filling in a couple of hours on the evening of your arrival, and you can also put in some good practice on the big slab on the right.

Your next venture might well be the Y Gully and Notch Arête, on the West Face of Tryfan. The pitches in the Y Gully are safe and easy to avoid and will teach you something about gullies. At the top of the gully you work left to the Notch Arête, which is most enjoyable. It is all rough grey rock and gets the afternoon and evening sun. It brings you out high up on the North Ridge of Tryfan, whence a pleasing scramble leads to the summit.

Then there is the Cneifion Arête, which rises out of the wild Nameless Cwm and reminds one of an Alpine ridge. It is broken by sharp pinnacles and holds a little loose rock, which gives good practice but need not be dangerous with a little care.

The Main Gully Ridge on Glyder Fach is also very pleasant. There is one difficult pitch near the top which you can easily avoid.

Now we can move over to Snowdon and have a look at the Parson's Nose. I took a novice up this climb last Easter, my first visit for several years, and it delighted me more than ever. The Nose itself is exposed, but the holds are good ; we were in cloud on this portion. Then we crossed the 15-foot gap and half-way up the ridge above we emerged from the mist into brilliant sunshine. We felt a great sense of height and isolation, looking down on a sea of swirling cloud, with the sunlit summits sticking out all around.

Some of the pitches on the ridge are quite awkward ; a delicate slab and a strenuous chimney in particular may give you some cause for thought. The ledges beneath are ample, however, and you won't hurt yourself if you do fall off.

These have all been moderate climbs. The Milestone Buttress has some harder pitches, though it cannot really be called difficult. It is splendid practice, because it possesses chimneys, walls, cracks, slabs, and a traverse. The holds are very big and consequently it is a muscular type of climb. Brute force will go a long way here. Like Little Tryfan this is ideal for a short evening, since it is less than ten minutes from the main road, from which the trails of white nailmarks that scar the various routes can be plainly seen. Make sure, though, that you stick to the Ordinary Route, since there are some very severe climbs on the Milestone.

If the Milestone goes well you may wish to wander up to the Heather Terrace and make the ascent of the North Buttress on the East Face of Tryfan. Some of the lower grooves are quite delicate, but when you have crossed the easy but exposed Terrace Wall on the upper part and sit on Belle Vue Terrace with your legs swinging in space, then you will be amply repaid.

If you want some practice in gullies—and your climbing education is not complete without—the North Gully on Tryfan is a typical specimen. The pitches are short, but strenuous and tricky. There is no danger of falling far, but you could easily hurt yourself. You will possibly get into some queer positions and tie yourself in knots before you emerge—triumphant, but stiff and dirty—at the top. You must take care that your feet or the rope (always blame it on the rope) do not dislodge any of the numerous loose stones lying about on to your companions below.

Another excellent practice ground is the West Buttress of Glyder Fach. The route is indefinite; the rock is sound and very rough. You can wander about at will, choosing chimneys, cracks or slabs, hard or easy as you wish. Dolmen Buttress, Route 1—on the same cliff—is also very suitable.

You should certainly pay a visit to the Idwal Slabs. The angle is easy but the belays are apt to be few and far between, so the leader should have 100 feet of rope. The Ordinary Route is quite simple, but when you have progressed a little further you can tackle Hope, which is a splendid climb of its standard.

In short, pick out any moderate climbs that sound attractive; when you feel at home on these promote yourself to the " difficults," and so on.

Personally I prefer Wales to the Lake District. Many people hold just as strongly to the opposite view. It is probably just a question of where you start. Each gives equally good rock-climbing, but the Welsh mountains certainly are real mountains; there are no sharp rocky peaks in the Lake District to compare with Tryfan or Crib Goch. On the other hand the Lakeland valleys are more beautiful.

Langdale and Coniston are the most easily reached Lakeland centres. Langdale has not much to offer the raw novice. Some of the Pavey Ark gullies are not difficult, but they are wet and rather loose. A few years ago a young lady was taken there for her first climb. She was standing at the bottom of one of the pitches when she was suddenly carried down the gully by a shower of stones and had her ankle so badly broken that several operations were necessary. However, it all ended happily, for she married one of the members of the party.

Middlefell Buttress is a pleasant and popular route, and there are some good short climbs on Scout Crag. Most of the other Langdale courses are rather difficult, however. Gimmer Crag is a wonderful piece of rock, but it is certainly no place for novices.

Coniston is the centre for Dow Crags, and here you will find infinite scope. For the Lakes you will need the Guides issued by the Fell and Rock Climbing Club. You will be able to pick out quite a number of moderate climbs on Dow Crags, and they are nearly all good.

The best centre of all is Wasdale Head, where you have Scafell, Great Gable, and Pillar Rock.

Scafell is the playground of the experts, but you can safely attempt such climbs as Broad Stand, Deep Ghyll, and Mickledore Chimney. After a little practice you will feel equal to Scafell Pinnacle by Professor's Chimney and Scafell Pinnacle by Slingsby's Chimney, which is a grand climb.

THE NEEDLE ARÊTE, GREAT GABLE.

This is a splendid route for climbers of limited experience.

You will find a great deal to occupy you on the Napes, that grand collection of sharp ⁚ 'ges jutting out from the steep scree slopes of Great Gable. The Arrowhead Ridge (easy way), the Eagle's Nest (West Chimney), and the Needle Arête should soon come within your powers, but it may be some time before you feel ready for the famous Napes Needle.

Pillar Rock is rather more distant, but it is a fine cliff; in fact it is really a peak on its own. The Slab and Notch Route and the Old West Route will be your first choices here, and then you can work through the moderates. When you are able to manage the North Climb and the New West you will have gained a great reward.

The Scafell and Great Gable climbs can be reached from Langdale if you don't mind a three-hours' walk. Borrowdale is nearer, but not so close as Wasdale. You will find generally that you have to walk much farther for your climbing in the Lakes than in Wales.

If you visit Scotland you will have to walk farther still. Glencoe and Fort William (for Ben Nevis) are the best centres, on the mainland anyhow. Many of the climbs are almost of Alpine length—anything up to 2,000 feet. But if you can get to the Isle of Skye, that is the best of all. Here you need a real mountaineering technique if you are to get up many of the peaks at all, even by the easiest routes. Guide-books for all these districts are issued by the Scottish Mountaineering Club.

I have been able to give you only a very brief

idea of what to do in the various districts ; the rest you must find out from the Guides. If you start off with the easiest climbs you will soon discover what you can do in safety.

You may feel a little nervous on your first lead. The thing to do is to forget about the height. When you are crossing a street you aren't frightened of the cars ; you know they won't hurt you unless you walk in front of them. Similarly the height won't hurt you unless you fall off ; and you won't fall off unless you let go with both hands. Concentrate on the holds and don't worry about what is below you.

Whatever else you do, don't trust to luck. Work out every move beforehand, and if things don't go as you expect come down and have another think. If you still don't feel sure that you can manage it in safety, give it up. It is no disgrace to turn back ; but it is a definite disgrace to fall off, whether you hurt yourself or not. Bad climbers often ascend by a series of rushes. If their rush does not carry them far enough they are lost ; they cannot remember any of the holds, and they come down with an even greater rush. So try and remember which holds you have used, and don't ascend a difficult stretch unless you are sure you can get down again if necessary.

As leader it is your job to get the party safely up the climb, or, failing that, to get it safely off the climb. All decisions rest in your hands ; if you decide to turn back no one must argue. Never bring your second up to a stance without a belay.

That is why it is so necessary to have sufficient rope. You must not fall off; but you must also make sure that if by some mischance you do, you won't pull your second off as well. Therefore you must always see that he is securely belayed before you start up a pitch.

Now, what is the second's job? He must safeguard the leader and he must encourage him. Above all he must show complete confidence in his leader. A good second is a terrific moral support. A nervous second, who will keep on worrying, has just the opposite effect. I have often felt quite shaky on a climb well within my powers, just because the man below would keep wondering what the next pitch was like—"How much more is there? Is there anything harder ahead?"—until I have become a mass of nerves myself. The only thing in such a case is to be really rude; if you can get the man annoyed he will cease to be frightened.

How different is a really good second! His confidence seems to flow into you and give you strength. You know he feels sure that you will get up in the end and does not mind how long he is kept waiting.

Old books on climbing often recommend having the leader's rope running over a spike of rock. This is a most dangerous practice. It will save the second's hands if the leader falls, but it may cost the leader his life, since the rope will almost certainly break over the spike. The leader may himself put the rope over a spike for a short difficult section, but as soon as he is more than 5 or 6 feet above it, it becomes a source of danger. A leader falling from 40 feet above his second may eventually be held, but if he falls 20 feet with the rope running over a sharp edge—then, snap goes the rope.

There is one tip I have not mentioned. On walls and slabs the lower part of the leg, below the knee, should almost always be kept vertical. If you have to raise your foot on to a high side-hold, don't keep the leg straight and all at an angle of 45 degrees ; bend the knee to a right-angle, so that the thigh is horizontal and the lower leg vertical.

What if you feel giddy on heights ? Can you hope ever to become a climber ?

Giddiness is usually curable. One method is to climb up a ladder and see how many rungs you can ascend before you begin to feel giddy. Then come down and have another try. Each time you will get a little farther. In the end it will seem ridiculous that you should feel dizzy at twenty-two rungs and not dizzy at twenty—a difference of a mere 12 inches —and you will succeed in reaching the top of the ladder. When you come down keep your eyes on the rungs and not on the ground ; I don't want to have your death on my conscience. You may not be cured immediately, but you will gradually improve. Actually the easier rock-climbs are too broken-up to make you giddy ; you get much more of a sensation of sheerness in looking down from the roof of a high building.

You may perhaps have noticed that I have made no special mention of climbing for girls and ladies. There has been no need, really, since they are included in everything that I have said. But there are one or two special points. I have given a lecture to a girls' school—four hundred of them and an eagle-eyed (and probably no less keen-eared) headmistress, watching to see that I did not say anything unsuitable for the ears of her tender charges—and I must say that I feel much happier writing to you than talking to you.

Firstly, make sure that you can hold the weight of a climber below you. Most girls, as soon as a strain comes on the rope, double up like a wilting flower. I don't know why they do so; perhaps they think they look more graceful that way. So pay very special attention to practising beforehand on trees or low rocks. Another thing—girls often seem to think that if they have a man as second they can fall from any height and he will hold them.

There are some very good lady climbers who can compete with any but first-class men on delicate stuff; on strenuous work, however, they are not usually so successful. Ladies, of course, more often follow than lead, and they should therefore take great pains to make themselves efficient seconds. There is, however, a club for women alone—the Pinnacle Club—which has many fine ascents to its credit.

Mountains unfortunately attract bad weather, so

you must learn to climb under all conditions. Don't be a fair-weather climber. It may seem strange, but I have derived as much enjoyment from days of streaming rocks and cold driving sleet as from the most comfortable conditions. You get a terrific thrill out of such ascents. You feel that you are battling against the elements, and the valleys and towns seem even farther away than usual, with their harmless showers and winds, that can do no more than annoy you.

You must have sufficient clothing in bad weather. When cold water is running down the rock—perhaps one day science will find a way of having it electrically heated—the greatest difficulty is to keep the fingers warm. So carry a pair of woollen gloves and also leather mitts. On the easier pitches you can wear the woollen gloves. Wear the mitts in between the pitches, while you are looking after the rope on stances. Never climb with cold fingers. Even if you are half-way up a pitch swing your arms about or put your hands in your pockets until feeling returns. If necessary, descend to the stance to do this.

Another thing you will need is a balaclava helmet. This is a woolly cap that is normally worn like any other hat, on top of the head. In cold conditions it can be pulled right down over the ears, so that only the face is exposed.

A high wind is always very trying. On anything at all delicate it is difficult to judge the moves with any degree of accuracy. Strenuous climbs, such as chimneys, where delicacy is less important than brute strength, are less seriously affected.

You will find that water makes the handholds very slippery, especially if the rock is inclined to be mossy. The footholds, on the other hand, are affected little or not at all. You can generally reckon that bad weather makes any climb about one standard harder ; a moderate route becomes difficult ; a difficult becomes a very difficult.

Still worse is wet snow. This has to be cleared from every hold and often makes a climb quite impossible.

Then there is ice. If there is only a little it may be cleared with an ice-axe or even a penknife ; if the rocks are badly glazed serious climbing is out of the question.

When you finally get on to the harder climbs— the severes and very severes—you will have learnt far more from your own experience than I can tell you. However, you may be interested to know something about the advanced routes ; it will give you some idea of what you are aiming at.

You will be impressed with the smallness of the stances, which are sometimes scarcely large enough for one foot. But this does not matter if the belay is good. You may be very uncomfortable, but you will be safe. Things are apt to be awkward when the second arrives and it is necessary to change places. He should, if possible, put on his belay before you take off yours. Then you may be able to move on a couple of steps, so as to keep out of his way while he adjusts his belay. On such a small stance, of course, you will be more or less suspended from the belay.

Sometimes there is a belay, but no stance. In such a case you may have to make a rope-cradle—a couple of loops in which to sit, with perhaps an extra one for the feet. Changing places with your second will be much easier if you are using a separate piece of rope for your loops.

Such methods are used on the famous Flake Crack, the most difficult pitch on the very severe Central Buttress of Scafell, one of the most exacting of British climbs.

The Flake Crack is 70 feet in height and quite vertical ; the final 12-foot section overhangs considerably. As the whole thing is half-way up a 400-foot cliff you can imagine how terrifically exposed it is.

The usual method of ascent is for one member of the party to make the very severe climb to the foot of the overhanging top portion. Then he ties on to the chockstone, sitting in two loops, with his feet in a third—leaning backwards over 200 feet of thin air.

Up comes the other man, who climbs first on to his companion's legs, then his shoulders, then his head. His hands are now only 3 or 4 feet from the top of the crack—so near and yet so far. Then follows 4 feet of desperate struggling—right leg jammed in the crack, left leg continually slipping out and hanging helplessly in the air, hands clutching feverishly at the rough rock. Your arms get tired and weak. Another few inches to the finishing hold—can you hang on ? At last ! Got it ! You have done it. No words can describe the thrill you feel as you sit astride the sharp edge of the flake, triumphant, looking down the sheer dizzy wall of rock.

When I did " C.B." (as it is called for short) my companion had his loops too small and consequently was too high up. I could kneel on his legs but could not manage to gain his shoulder. I was trampling about over his sagging body for fully an hour before I finally did get up. He was so covered with bruises that he could hardly walk next day.

There have been many startling adventures on the Flake Crack. One climber faced right instead of left and was unable to reach the final handhold. Instead he fell off. He hit the " Oval " 70 feet below, bounced off, and struck another ledge just as the rope tightened. It did not break and he was only slightly hurt, but the other man had his shoulders and hands badly torn and burnt with the friction of the rope. It was with great difficulty that he managed the painful business of abseiling down.

A climb of such difficulty is done not in boots, but in rubbers. These are ordinary plimsolls or gym shoes. Get a pair with rubber soles—not crêpe. The cheaper and lighter they are, the better. You will not be using them for walking—you change from boots at the foot of the climb—and if the soles are too thick you cannot feel the holds so well. Wear them with only one pair of stockings and see that they fit very tightly ; they are useless if there is a lot of empty space in the toe.

You will find that rubbers will grip on the smallest and most sloping holds. Well, why not wear them always, you may say. The answer is that they have one serious disadvantage ; they are no use on anything but perfectly dry rock. On grass, or on wet or muddy rock, they are highly dangerous. Also they are useless for general mountaineering ; they are uncomfortable for walking, and on snow or ice you might just as well be wearing skates. So begin with the standard mountaineering footwear—nailed boots. If you have done all your climbing in rubbers it is hard to get into the way of using boots ; but rubbers will seem all the better for your being used to boots. The easier climbs are actually just as safe and rather more interesting in boots ; also you do not have the bother of changing and of keeping your feet dry on the climb.

Scarpetti — rope-soled shoes, originally used chiefly in the Dolomites—are coming into favour in this country. They are equally good on wet or dry rocks and are cheaper to buy than boots. On most rock they grip rather better too. However, they wear out quickly and prove more expensive in the long run. Also they are too light to be really comfortable on long walks or scrambles.

You will have to get used to long run-outs—so

or 100 feet, or more. When you are a matter of 100 feet or so above your second, the rope cannot possibly help you if you fall. All the same it is amazing what a comfort it is ; you feel you have some connection with the rest of the party.

This is when you appreciate having a light line, instead of a heavy rope. You will also have to use some very small belays, for which line is much more convenient.

You must learn the technique of dealing with grass and loose rock, which need not always be dangerous if you treat them with respect. The thing is to divide your weight evenly between all your limbs ; never have it all on one foot or one hand. Then, if a hold does give way, you still have three points of support left.

Quite often you will be out of sight of your second, and if there is a wind blowing it may be impossible for you to hear each other. You must arrange that he is not to start climbing until the rope has been taut for at least ten seconds. Then there is no risk of his coming up before you are ready to hold him.

Then there is the question of your own rope. If you think that you have run it nearly all out on a long lead, and it is too windy for you to hear your second's shouts, you must pull in all the slack to see how much farther you can go in safety. You don't want to risk being pulled up—and possibly off—with a jerk.

There is one more important point—learn to

climb down from the very beginning of your career. You must be able to return in safety in case of emergency, and obviously you will be no good in the Alps if you can climb only uphill. You can almost always walk down easily by the side of any British cliffs; but make a point of descending at least half as many climbs as you ascend.

In a descent the leader goes down last, but the first man down has a certain responsibility in finding the route. It is a mistake to imagine that going down is necessarily more difficult than going up. It is probably true enough for anything delicate, such as slabs; but strenuous chimneys and steep walls are often much easier in descent. It is apt to be rather alarming starting off. Usually the best way is to sit on your ledge at the top, place your hands, both on the same side of you, on the rock, and then let yourself down over the edge. Footholds will appear to be much farther away than they actually are; it is surprising what a distance you can reach when hanging full-length from your hands.

Belays and stances are used exactly as for an ascent, of course; but now it is the lowest man's job to select suitable stopping-places.

Finally, never climb beyond your standard. Do not rush suddenly to a severe climb when you have never done anything but difficults before. Work gradually up the scale of difficulty, climb carefully and always be prepared to turn back.

Chapter VII

BRITISH SNOW-CLIMBING

I WAS on Snowdon one New Year's Day—1938, I think it was. There was very little snow about; from below it had not looked as though we should need our axes. When we got above Glaslyn, however, we found the middle Trinity Gully quite well filled with good hard snow, and had a pleasant bout of step-cutting.

We descended by the zigzags down to Glaslyn, an ordinary tourist route in summer. Now, it was impossible to descend without crossing a certain amount of hard snow. A little way down was a large and rather worried party, judging by all the shouting that was going on. They had come up equipped for a pleasant stroll and had got into trouble.

They had all descended separate tongues of frozen stones until they found themselves cut off by hard snow. So there they all were, each one marooned on his own little island of stones. They could move comfortably enough on the scree, but could not keep their footing on the hard snow.

One of them, bolder than the rest, made an effort to descend the snow. He succeeded. His feet shot from under him and he slid down with increasing velocity on his back. His feet caught on a rock and he was jerked upright and by a great effort managed to prevent himself from falling forward on to his face. He fell back again on another patch of snow and once more succeeded in regaining a standing position. There he was, running down the scree quite out of control, going faster and faster and having to take longer and longer strides to keep himself from pitching on to his face. Somehow he kept his balance and at last managed to stop.

Naturally the rest of the party did not feel very much encouraged by this performance. So we hurried to their aid and spent a hot half-hour cutting bucket-like steps for them. We were in no hurry and found the whole thing rather amusing.

Now, apart from the risk, you don't want to make a fool of yourself in this way. Therefore, when there is snow about, never venture on the mountains without an ice-axe.

The best axes are made abroad—in Switzerland, France, and Austria—but can be bought in this country. Before the war they cost from £1 to 30s. Buy a good heavy pattern, weighing about 3 pounds. Lighter axes are made and are useful when there is rock-climbing to be done, but heavier ones are better for step-cutting, especially for a long spell.

As you can see from the illustration opposite page 79, the head of the axe has a spike at one end and a hatchet-shaped edge (the edge being horizontal, not vertical) at the other. The spike is used for cutting steps in ice, the axe-blade for snow. I like a head about 12 inches in length, but that is largely a matter of personal taste. The under edge of the ice-cutting part should be straight, but the snow-cutting blade may be slightly curved. For the edge of this blade 2½ inches is quite a good average width.

Many axes have teeth notched underneath the ice-cutting pick. These teeth are meant to help in splitting the ice, so that the axe does not jam. They are said to be incorrect, but do not actually seem to do much harm.

The axe should balance 9 inches from the head. However, I have a favourite axe which balances nearly a foot from the head and yet cuts very well. So this point also is largely a matter of taste. I advise you to get some expert help in choosing your axe, if possible. Buy one that swings nicely and does not feel like a lump of lead on a piece of string. If you get a good make you should not go far wrong.

Your ice-axe should not come higher than the hip-bone, and when supported by both ends should bend only slightly when you hang from the middle. You will see later on how important this is.

Many experts do not use an ice-axe sling. They hang on by instinct, whatever may happen. There are many tales of Continental stars who have been killed by terrific falls, and have been found, still clutching on to the broken remains of their axes.

The loss of an axe may be so serious, especially in the Alps, that I always like to have some kind of sling.

The ordinary loop, attached to the head of the axe, is a great nuisance when cutting ; it flaps about and distracts the eye, and also soon gets cut. Therefore, a loop on a ring that slides up and down the shaft is indicated. But we need something to stop it from sliding right off the bottom of the shaft. One method is to have the ring tied to the head of the axe by a cord about 2½ feet long ; this will allow the ring to slide, but will prevent it from running off the end. It is rather apt, however, to get twisted and be a nuisance. The most common way is to have a metal band near the bottom of the shaft. This makes probing difficult in very hard snow. I recommend you, therefore, to buy an axe that has a shaft that is the same width all the way down. Get a circular ring of stout brass that will just slide comfortably on the shaft. All you will need to stop the ring coming off will be two very small screws, which will not interfere with probing.

You can now attach your sling to this ring. A 2-foot length of picture-cord does very well. Tie it so that the loop for the wrist is about 6 inches away from the ring, and see that you make the loop large enough to go over your leather mitts. Thin lamp-wick, also, makes a good sling, but this must be sewn on.

At the bottom of the ice-axe shaft you will notice a strong iron spike. This is used for belaying in snow and for probing for crevasses ; it also protects the wood, of course.

There have been quite a number of deaths from exposure even on our own little mountains. Not accidents—the victims have just lain down in the snow and died. The cause—faulty or inadequate clothing or shortage of food.

Remember that you may get almost Arctic conditions on the British hills in winter. Or you may get a hot sun blazing down on to the snow. One March day I climbed in rubbers on Bochlwyd Buttress, sat and baked in the sun, without my shirt, beside the frozen Llyn Bochlwyd, and then waded through three feet of snow up to the summit of Glyder Fach. So you must be prepared for extremes.

Your clothing should be windproof—thin windproof trousers over flannel bags and wind-jacket over woollen sweaters. Several thin sweaters are much warmer than one thick one ; Shetland wool is ideal. Short puttees are useful to keep the snow out of the boots. They should be wound round the ankle only—not round the calf or they will tend to stop the circulation, which is the surest road to frostbite. A balaclava helmet and leather mitts complete the outfit.

Unless it is very cold you will not need all this equipment, but you should bring sufficient spares with you. It may seem warm enough in the valleys, but a biting wind or a blizzard on the tops will completely change the outlook.

You should carry also a pocket torch and spare battery, and remember to take an ample supply of food.

We will now make an ascent of the middle Trinity Gully, which runs up the northern face under the summit of Snowdon.

You don't come across much snow below Glaslyn, but as soon as you reach the lake you are in a world of white. By contrast Glaslyn looks as black as ink, except for the encircling rim of ice. It is a lovely day towards the end of February. The sky is of the deepest blue and the snow is dazzling in the sunshine, though in the shade the air is quite keen.

You start up the zigzags and then strike off to the left into the hollow basin immediately below the crags. Then you start up the snow-slope.

The snow is so hard that you cannot kick steps. However, the angle is easy at first and you can walk quite comfortably. Then it steepens and your feet begin to slip, so you cut a few steps. There is no danger so you don't put on the rope yet.

You cut in zigzags — not straight up. When you are cutting up to the right, hold the middle of the shaft with the right hand and the bottom end with the left. The hands are reversed for cutting to the left. Use the blade of the axe. Cut with a swinging stroke, and when the axe strikes the snow pull it towards you, so that a long step is scraped out. This needs a lot of practice to do neatly with one blow, but when you are used to it you will find it easier to cut then to kick steps if the snow is at all inclined to be hard.

Cut your steps close together and arrange them in the right place for the feet. This is not quite so easy as it sounds. Imagine you are working up to the right on a fairly steep slope. You cut one step for the right foot. Cut the step for the left foot immediately above this. The next step for the right foot is then made to the right of the left footstep and on the same level. Similarly, if you are working up to the left, the right foot uses the higher line of steps.

At the end of each zigzag make an extra large step for turning. You should never need to stretch to reach from one step to the next; if the steps are correctly cut your feet will fall naturally into them.

You are now at the top of the open slope and have reached the foot of the gully itself. You decide to rope up. Normally you would not need more than 25 feet on snow, but there may be some awkward bits ahead, so you allow yourself 40 feet. Your second ties on 40 feet from the end and coils the remainder round his shoulder, or, better still, puts it in his rucksack, where it won't be in the way.

You must now take up some of the rope in coils, which you carry in one hand, and No. 2 must do the same. There are three reasons for this. Firstly it gets surplus rope out of the way; secondly it prevents jerking, as the second can let out a coil or two if the rope begins to get tight; and thirdly, if one falls off the strain comes more gradually on to the other. It is a nuisance carrying coils when you are cutting, but it has to be done.

You now proceed. It is the second's job to see that the rope neither jerks nor gets too slack. He should keep about 15 feet behind the leader.

The snow is steeper now and needs two blows to each step. The second should drive the shaft of his axe into the snow—to the head if possible—between each step. Every time he does this the party is securely belayed.

Cut with a steady rhythm, not in jerks. You will find it very hot work. To help you to keep your balance in stepping up you may drive the pick of your axe into the snow.

Half-way up you come to a little chockstone pitch. It is almost buried in snow, but you can just see down into a black hole. Here the snow gives way to ice for a short distance, so you bring up your second. He digs out a stance, belays himself by driving his axe into the snow and winding the rope round the shaft, and pays out your rope as in rock-climbing.

You use the pick of your axe for the ice and find that each step needs about ten or fifteen blows —it isn't very hard ice. Quite often you have nearly completed a step, give it one more finishing touch— and smash it to smithereens. You must hit hard, but you must also hit accurately. You can use the blade of the axe to clear out your step. Ice-steps must always slope slightly inwards, and it is important to make them big enough—and especially, long enough.

The gully gets narrower now, and you have to be constantly turning. You are very grateful for the sliding sling, which works equally well whether you are cutting to the right or to the left, and can be kept all the time on the same wrist.

One little pitch is so narrow that you have to cut the steps one above the other, like a ladder. You get your second to belay again and hold your rope for this bit, but soon you are both able to move together once more.

The slope is much steeper than it appeared from below—about 50 degrees, actually, though it seems more. You realize that on snow and ice it is even more important to stand upright, away from the slope, than on rock.

You watch lumps of snow go sliding down and gain some idea of what would happen to you if you were so foolish as to follow suit. It looks a long, long way, down the narrow ribbon of the gully and out to the curving slopes below.

Up here all the rocks are covered with ice, blown into beautiful, delicate feathery plumes. Everything is white—the whole world.

The gully opens out at the top, like a fan. You emerge from the narrow funnel on to a broad slope. It is a relief to have room to cut fifty steps or more without turning.

You can see the ridge, quite close above ; it is protected by an alarming cornice, which looks dead and cold underneath, but transparent where the sun catches the edge. The sky is very blue; you can see little white clouds drifting beyond the cornice. You feel a sudden longing to be on the ridge, sitting in the sun, all difficulty and worry left behind.

The cornice curves over gracefully and overhangs about 3 feet. The slope below is almost vertical for the last 8 feet. You bring your second up as high as possible, see that he is firmly belayed, tell him to be ready to hold you, and set off on the last and most difficult lap.

Close to the cornice the snow is much softer and you are able to keep your balance by plunging in the left arm, up to the shoulder. You dig yourself in and prepare to tackle the overhang. You obviously cannot climb it, so you must remove it. You gingerly hit the edge of the cornice, well away to the right, so that it won't fall on you. A large lump falls on to your second. The silly chap doesn't seem to like it. You gradually cut away the cornice, until it is no longer an overhang. It is most exhausting work, because you are cutting with one hand, and above you as well. Your arm is aching, so you stop for a rest. You take a look at your second. He is half-buried in snow, and shivering. It seems strange, since you are soaked in perspiration.

You enlarge the gap until you have hacked out a recess, into which you think you can squeeze. You now plunge in your axe, as high up as possible,

A SNOW-CORNICE ON BEN NEVIS.

Not a very difficult specimen. The leader is playing the second's rope round his ice-axe, dug firmly
into the snow.

put your full weight on it, haul up until you can get your knees into the recess, and emerge dramatically, if breathlessly, on to the level ridge. The sight of the half-buried railway line adds a vulgar touch.

There is a great deal more in snow-craft than in rock-climbing, so I can give you only a bare idea of what you can learn on the homeland hills. The first thing is to know how to stop yourself in case of a slip. Choose a safe slope of hard snow—some place where it won't matter if you fail to stop. Lie on your back and begin sliding. Have one hand over the head of the axe, and the other round the shaft, just below the head. Turn over on to your face, with the axe held firmly under the chest, so that the pick digs into the snow. It is amazing how quickly you can pull yourself up in this way. But it needs great coolness to apply if you are moving fast down a dangerous slope, so you cannot have too much practice beforehand. If you are sliding head-first or (worst of all) rolling, all you can do is to try and work yourself into the right position. Provided you hang on to your axe you have a good chance. I once managed to stop myself after sliding, out of control, for 400 feet. It is in such an emergency that a sling is invaluable. If you lose your axe all you can do is to lie on your back and try and dig in your heels and fingers.

One little tip—wear gloves while you are practising, otherwise you will skin your hands.

Special methods are required for traversing. If

the snow is soft you should either drive in the shaft above you or hold the axe across the front of the body, with the head away from the slope, and keep the spiked end dug into the snow during each move. If the snow is hard the axe is still held across the body, but the pick is driven into the snow.

The next thing to learn is the technique of descent. Cutting steps downhill is not very easy at first. You are working with the full length of the axe, which means that you have a longer swing and must aim more accurately. The balance, too, is more difficult ; a badly mistimed stroke might possibly swing you off your steps.

The first man down cuts the steps and the last man is largely responsible for holding the party ; thus neither should be entirely inexperienced.

Another thing to learn is glissading. This is a quick method of descent, to be used only on safe slopes. To put it simply, you just stand on your feet and slide. The axe is used to help you to keep your balance, so that you don't finish up on your back. Hold one hand over the head of the axe, hold the shaft near the middle with the other, and have the spike just touching the snow behind you. To stop, dig in your heels and push the axe into the snow. If you do fall down you will gain speed rapidly and should immediately turn over on to your axe to stop yourself. After a good deal of practice it is possible to steer with your feet when doing a standing glissade.

If the snow is too soft for a standing glissade

you can do a sitting glissade. This method should be used with caution, since you have not nearly so much control.

A long slope of steep ice is very exhausting. Each step may require thirty blows of the axe, and there is more danger than on snow of swinging yourself out of your steps. You cannot ever relax on ice; even standing still in your holds is a constant strain. Neither can you belay with any certainty. The best you can do is drive the pick of your axe into the ice, choosing your spot so that when the pick is well in the bottom of the shaft is resting on a step—not an easy matter. No one must slip. However, you are not likely to come across many long slopes of this description in England or Wales.

What you may sometimes meet is a vertical wall of ice. Very often you can get a rock or ice-axe belay at the bottom, which will make it fairly safe. It is a long and laborious business. Handholds have to be cut, a process which needs the delicacy of a sculptor. They should be incut, so that you can get your fingers behind. Wear woollen gloves ; these freeze on to the ice and give a good grip. When at last you are clinging to the ice-wall with one hand and cutting steps with the other you may have to come down several times to rest.

A vertical 30-foot ice-wall will take over an hour to climb—quite possibly two hours or more. Frozen waterfalls make good practice-grounds.

Avalanches are rare on our homeland hills, but

do sometimes occur. I was once ascending the Ladies' Gully on Snowdon. It was snowing heavily and blowing a gale—a regular blizzard. A ceaseless stream of fine powdery snow, about six inches deep, was pouring down the gully. It was obviously being blown over from the top, since it increased after each extra strong gust. After a time it began to pile up and get heavy and dangerous, so I turned back. This was hardly worthy of being called an avalanche, but sometimes you get whole cornices crashing down ; this is not likely to occur until a thaw sets in. Last Easter a party was swept down a Ben Nevis gully by the collapse of an ice-wall, but luckily sustained no serious injury.

The best months for snow-climbing are February and March, but you can never be certain of it. Some years the mountains are white all through the winter ; other years there is hardly any snow at all. A good thing to know is that the temperature falls roughly 1 degree Fahrenheit for every 300 feet of height ; thus you can work out at what height it will be freezing.

If you go to Scotland, April and May are also often very good. By far the best British mountain for snow-work is Ben Nevis, which keeps a little of its snow all the year round. The conditions are often quite Alpine ; at Easter, in fact, they are usually positively Arctic.

Snow-craft cannot be learnt from a book. I have told you enough to enable you to tackle any of the ordinary pedestrian routes in winter. The rest you must learn by experience. As soon as you set foot on the crisp snow and see the dazzling summits all around you will be fired by an urge to do greater things. I have mentioned the more difficult problems, but only as a matter of interest; you must do the easier slopes and gullies first. Until you have had a slip, snow seems much safer than rock; the angle is so much easier. So take especial care.

You are now ready for the Alps—with a guide or a party of experienced amateurs.

CHAPTER VIII

FIRST ASCENTS

YOU do not need to go to the far corners of the earth to be an explorer. You can still find places in this country where no one has ever been before. But probably many people will have tried, so you will need to be a pretty good climber to reach them. But this does not necessarily follow; I found a good new climb on Craig yr Ysfa, the Amphitheatre Rib, that was no more than very difficult. Thousands of climbers had passed it without really noticing it; most of the people who visit Craig yr Ysfa do either the Great Gully or the Amphitheatre Buttress.

When I first started climbing I could think of nothing else. Cooped up all week in an office, I would just long for the next week-end. On a photograph of some cliff I would have all the known routes marked with dotted lines. The blank spaces in between fascinated me. Here was unexplored country; I longed to be the first to set foot upon it. I used to sit, pretending to work, with the drawer slightly open, so that I could see the photo inside. Then I would plan a route. Here was a chimney to start, but could I reach that little grass ledge 100 feet higher up ? It might be possible ; it all depended on the steepness of the rock. If I could find a way of connecting the next three ledges, then victory would be mine.

The first fine week-end I would put my theories into practice. Curiously enough, they usually worked. But it meant hours of suspense. I would go up, get stuck and have to come down again. Then I would try another way, until at last I found a route to the next ledge. Then the same thing would have to be gone through again, until finally I arrived triumphant at the top, with another new climb added to the cliffs of Wales.

On an old and popular climb there is little of the thrill of exploration. You know it is possible ; you are even told the route and the standard of difficulty. But on a new climb it is quite a different story. You should not make any move that you cannot reverse. Of course, people do ; that is how many severe first ascents are made. The climber comes to an impossible looking pitch. He says to himself, " I daren't descend that lower slab ; I must get up somehow." And usually he does. There is no doubt that greater risks are taken on new climbs. You feel that it is worth a fight. So it is ; but all the same it isn't worth while getting killed over it.

When you do a popular climb, like the Gashed Crag or the Milestone Buttress, you will think what a lucky thing it is that the rocks are so clean—no grass or soil or loose rock. But it isn't really just luck. You may be sure that when these climbs were first done they were covered with vegetation. So one of the chief jobs on a new climb is " gardening." This doesn't mean that you go about planting wallflowers and hollyhocks—just the opposite. You have to clear grass out of the holds and throw down loose rocks and insecure ledges, until you have made the place safe for yourself and future climbers. There are few more cheering sights than seeing your second half-buried under a large and slimy sod.

On Snowdon there is a cliff called Clogwyn d'ur Arddu. Its name is enough to frighten away many people. It is over 500 feet in height and mostly vertical—quite the most magnificent precipice in England and Wales. Up to 1931 there was only one route on each of the two main buttresses. It was the West Buttress that first attracted me. In 1927, Longland and Pigott and Morley Wood had succeeded in breaking across from the left, to make their magnificent West Buttress Route.

My friend, Dr. Graham Macphee, had led me in record time up this climb, and we were sun-bathing by the dark little Llyn d'ur Arddu. Macphee thought he had earned his rest, as indeed he had, but I had other ideas. I had designs on the middle of the West Buttress.

On the upper half of the buttress was a huge slab. If only it could be reached ! Below, the rocks were almost vertical. But the main problem was in the first few feet. All the way along the foot of the cliff the rocks overhung. It was a genuine overhang, too ; it formed a kind of covered corridor, with a roof that projected in places for 20 feet or more. Nobody had yet succeeded in overcoming this overhang. There seemed to be a faint chance in the middle, where a pile of blocks formed a kind of natural ladder. A well-known climber had tried to climb straight up at this point and had fallen off, luckily without hurting himself. It looked a nasty place, but it seemed to me that, instead of climbing upwards, it might be possible to traverse out to the left, above the overhang. This would lead to a narrow slab, which ran up to the skyline and out of sight. It was impossible to guess what happened after that.

The traverse was very severe. There was one sloping hold where my rubbers would not grip at all, so at last I took them off and managed to get across in my stockinged feet.

I found myself on a tiny grass ledge, looking rather hopelessly up at the grim face above. I had crossed on to a higher part of the cliff and was already about 100 feet above the bottom, with the overhang below me. I felt very small and isolated.

I started up the narrow slab. It was far more difficult than it had looked, and wickedly rotten. I threw down every other hold. A thin ribbon of grass ran all the way up on the right, looking like a long and ragged caterpillar. I thought that even this might be safer than the rock and plunged into it. It wasn't at all a friendly kind of caterpillar; it began to peel off and slide down. I left this moving staircase very hurriedly, and took to the rocks again. I climbed on the extreme edge, where it seemed to be a little firmer. Below my left foot the rocks dropped, sheer and unclimbable, for 200 feet.

Macphee called up that I had run out nearly all of the 120-foot line. There was no stance in sight, so I had to stand about uncomfortably while he tied on another 100-foot length. I went on and on, with things looking more and more hopeless. I wondered whether I should ever find a belay.

At last the climbing began to get easier, and I was able to traverse to a sheltered grassy recess on the left. There was a perfect thread-belay, and Macphee soon joined me. It was wonderful to think that no one had ever been here before. It was still more interesting to wonder whether we should ever escape.

I tried the slab immediately above, but did not dare to pass a big loose block, resting on a ledge. A few years later, an optimistic climber was more daring; he succeeded in pulling the block on top of himself, gashing his hand very badly. He had to abseil down, weak and faint from loss of blood. He got back very late, and search-parties were out all night looking for him. By this time he was safely in bed. Some one had made a muddle of things.

We climbed a rib to a little stance. The big

slab, for which we were aiming, was away on our right. It was very steep and smooth here; the far side looked much more hopeful. But could we reach it?

I got a long way across, and then stuck. The next move might be possible, by a kind of jump. It would be dangerous, but—well, a new climb was worth a risk. I looked at it a long time. It seemed to grow more and more grim. The exposure was terrifying and I was a long way from my second. I came back.

I managed to find an easier way across, at a lower level; but that meant that I still had the steep part of the slab ahead of me. The corner was a 20-foot wall of literally vertical grass. I made a mad rush at it. I had to climb up more quickly than the grass fell down. It was nasty and dangerous, but I dug in my finger-nails and toes (I was still climbing in stockings) and clutched and scrabbled until I reached the top. I don't know what Macphee thought of all this. He is a safe and careful climber himself. But he is an ideal second. He watches you carefully and says nothing, except to point out a hold now and again. You feel that he trusts you and expects you to get up, and so you jolly well do get up. Also, he is equally famous both as an Alpinist and as a rock-climber, so that I knew I could not have had a better man to back me up.

The next pitch was still grass, but not quite so steep. The turf split from the slab and curled up.

119

It was rather like standing on a roll of carpet—with the carpet going on unrolling. It was very difficult and unpleasant. But our reward was to come. We had two wonderful airy 100-foot pitches, right up and across the Great Slab, to its top left-hand corner. The rock was warm and very rough, and we felt profoundly happy and exhilarated. All the thrill of conquest was ours. The climbing was just severe, but it was easy after what had gone before and we seemed to glide up without effort.

Macphee said I deserved a kick in the pants or a potato medal, he didn't know which. Why only a potato medal I don't know ; I felt I deserved more than that. But it had been a marvellous day. We had done 1,000 feet of rock-climbing, most of it in the very severe class.

No one else can have the thrill of the first ascent. Climbers have now unearthed a spike so that the leader can be protected on the first traverse ; they have cleaned away the grass and loose rock, and even found a belay of sorts half-way up the first pitch. Nowadays, the hardest portions are the grass wall and the " carpet-roll " slab above. But the Great Slab Route is still very severe, and still one of the most magnificent climbs in the country.

You will see that a lot of the fun of a first ascent lies in the problem of finding the route. You get such surprises. Things that look impossible from below turn out to be covered with holds ; innocent-looking little slabs prove to be quite unclimbable.

We had a great deal of fun finding a way up the

A CRACK.

The first pitch of the very severe Curving Crack on Clogwyn d'ur Arddu. The ascent is made mainly by jamming the hands and feet.

[*Photo : Eileen Foster.*

AN ABSEIL.

Curving Crack, on the same cliff. We could not get up the bottom portion, which was a kind of smooth chimney, overhanging in places. A. W. Bridge, Alan Hargreaves, and I spent the best part of a day, giving each other shoulders in most perilous positions. Alf Bridge is a brilliant climber and enormously strong; his arms have saved him more than once on a desperate lead. He wedged himself 50 feet above the ground, and we took it in turns to try and climb over him. He kept up a constant stream of encouragement. " I've got you ; you're all right. I'll hold your feet and push you up, and you can make a jump for that hold. Of course I can hold you ; I could stay here for weeks."

But it was all no use ; there were no reasonable holds on the overhang. Alan was the lightest of the three, and Alf was really most anxious to try and throw him up. Alan did not seem to think it a very good idea.

We had given it up as a bad job when we heard a shout from above. We looked up, and there was Maurice Linnell at the top of our pitch. He had climbed a crack on the other side. It was such a ferocious-looking crack—very narrow, and over-hanging for most of its 40 feet—that we hadn't even tried it. We rushed up and found it much easier than it had looked, though very strenuous. Maurice very generously insisted on my leading. He said that it was my climb, since I had first thought of looking at it. He was a very fine climber and could tackle anything that was within my powers, so it was a most unselfish action. It was typical of him.

I don't suggest that you should start off with climbs such as these. By the time you are fit for them you won't need a book to tell you what to do. But it is a pleasure to me to live these adventures over again, and I hope that I have succeeded in passing on to you some idea of the excitement and enjoyment they have given me.

CHAPTER IX

BIVOUACS

ISN'T it boring sleeping every night in a bed ?
Don't you sometimes long for a change ?
Wouldn't you like to lie and see the stars above
you, or sleep like a polar bear in the snow ?
Possibly not—you think it sounds too cold. But it
need not be ; with correct equipment you can keep
warm under the most severe conditions.

One winter's night I cycled up to a climbers'
cottage in the Ogwen Valley. The place was
empty and locked-up when I arrived. The key
was at the farm ; but it was after midnight and I
did not want to waken them, so I decided to sleep
out in the open.

It was a cold night—cold enough to freeze the
stream. I put on all my clothes and looked around
for a suitable site. The only sheltered spot seemed
to be the rubbish dump, which was enclosed on
three sides. So I lay down amongst the tins.
Luckily the smells also were frozen up.

The greatest discomfort was the large stone
which I had for a pillow. Now and again, when I
began to feel chilled, I would stroll about a little.
I was never miserably cold, and managed to get

quite a fair amount of sleep. I felt fresh enough in the morning.

It was a lovely day and two of us spent the next night in sleeping-bags on the top of Snowdon. We slept in the snow, in 12 degrees of frost, but our bags kept us as warm as toast.

These were bivouacs. If you drag a large tent out of a car and sleep in camp beds, that may be camping, but it is not bivouacking. A bivouac is a resting-place for the night. Sometimes it enables you to do a climb that is too far away from ordinary sleeping places ; sometimes, in an emergency, it is just a case of somehow keeping alive until the morning. But I like to bivouac for the fun of the thing. It is grand to wander over the mountains with a sleeping-bag, never having to worry about the time, just lying down in the snow when it gets dark.

You will need a good eiderdown sleeping-bag to do this. The colder it is, within reason, the better. If it is below freezing-point you won't get wet, even if it snows. The snow underneath you will keep dry as well. But if it isn't freezing, and there is any chance of rain or wet snow, you will need a light tent as well. Special bivouac tents are made, with wide flaps, so that they can be fastened down with stones.

Snow is uncomfortable stuff to sleep upon ; it soon turns to ice underneath you, and gets almost as lumpy as a Welsh farmhouse bed. But you will have to put up with these little hardships.

I have camped many times by Clogwyn d'ur Arddu, that grandest of Welsh cliffs. It is wonderful seeing the moonlight on the crags ; they look huge and ghostly, and every detail stands out in the silvery light. We used to pitch our tent right beneath the rocks, and the top looked like a jagged ridge of pinnacles, towering up into the sky. We felt ready for anything after such a night—even a new climb on " Cloggy."

I had a very enjoyable camp once in the Nameless Cwm, on the Glyders. We pitched the little tent on a flat patch of snow just below the grim cliff of Clogwyn Du. Everything was perfect. It was freezing, but there was a little stream just managing to run, part of the way underneath the hard snow. We squatted outside the tent and looked at the dark shadow that was the Nant Ffrancon Valley, lit only by the shiny winding line of the river. It was hard to believe that we were anywhere near civilization ; we could forget all about the world, except that wild and glorious part of it which was close around.

One snowy night two of my friends were bivouacking on the top of y Garn, one of the Welsh " three-thousanders." A party of us decided that it would be a good idea to take them up some hot coffee. Why they should want hot coffee, I don't know ; they had plenty of provisions with them. But we were determined that they should have hot coffee, whether they wanted it or not. We were going out on a noble pilgrimage. The fact of the matter was that it was such a marvellous night that we had to have an excuse to venture out.

Above the little lake there was nothing but snow to be seen. We sat down, hot and glowing, and could almost feel the frozen silence. It was strange to hear no sound at all; even the streams were still.

The snow was brilliant in the moonlight and step-cutting was a simple matter. It was more difficult in the shadow, because it was almost impossible to make out any detail. It was good practice, cutting by feel. Part of the time I worked with an electric torch held in my mouth.

Bob and Charles were just getting off to sleep when we reached their tent at 2 a.m. They seemed to think they could have survived without us. We were so exhausted with our noble efforts that we had to drink most of the coffee ourselves. We helped it down with some of the campers' food; we thought it would save them the trouble of carrying it down. They were really quite polite about it; I think they were too sleepy to make a fuss.

Another time I had a lone sleeping-bag bivouac on the summit of y Garn, without a tent. It was windy on the open slope, and the only sheltered spot was close to the cairn. Here, however, the snow was rather steep, and all night I was afraid of sliding and possibly going over the precipitous northern edge. You feel very helpless in a sleeping-bag; your arms are tucked snugly inside and you would slide a long way before you could start to save yourself.

I had no windproof cover to my sleeping-bag and did not keep very warm. A thick damp cloud was all around, and a chilly wind was blowing. I descended with the first signs of the grey depressing dawn.

One of my most interesting bivouacs was on Snowdon. It was the coldest day of that winter, though it was well on into March. After getting out of the car, my ears were completely numb before I had walked fifty yards along the road.

We set out about nine o'clock at night. The ground was frozen hard, and it was bitterly cold. We walked briskly, and soon got warm.

We were really going out to test some new sleeping-bags, specially designed for the Himalaya. We also wanted to see whether we could build a snow-house or igloo, after the Eskimo fashion.

Above Glaslyn the snow was deep and fairly hard. It was quite tense work, cutting steps in the darkness and cloud, with the gale swirling the snow violently into our faces. We also had the Alpine danger of crevasses, for there are some disused copper-mines above Glaslyn that often get completely bridged by snow.

There was an absolute blizzard raging when we arrived on the ridge between y Wyddfa and Crib-y-Ddisgyl. There were 18 degrees of frost. In an experimental mood I put my tongue on to my ice-axe and nearly got it frozen on.

We worked feverishly, cutting blocks out of the hard snow to build our house. I am afraid it would not have passed a town-planning director ; it blew down almost as fast as we built it up, sometimes faster. Perhaps it was like some of the " desirable modern residences—all conven., h. and c."—which won't stand a wind until they have the support of the wallpaper.

All we managed to do was to build a low semi-circular wall, rather like a sheep-shelter. I was last in bed, and I ran round and round the encampment in an effort to keep warm. Little particles of ice were being whipped stingingly into my face ; the wind was shrieking and howling, and the snow and cloud were being driven along in a smoky fury. My clothes were frozen stiff as boards and covered with hoar-frost.

With numb fingers I took off my boots and squirmed into the bag. My boots came in with me, clogged with snow as they were. I knew how impossible it was to put on frozen boots in the morning.

The opening over the face fastened up with press-fasteners. In a later pattern we used zipps. I had to warm my fingers several times before I could get the whole thing done up. I found it hard to breathe at first and thought I was going to suffocate ; I felt as if I were in a coffin. The sensation soon passed ; actually it was quite easy to breathe through the down.

I " dined " inside my bag, with the aid of a torch. All the food was frozen solid and seemed to have completely lost its taste. I was enjoying a slab of cake ; I shone the light on it and it turned out to be corned beef.

Our bags had shiny black waterproof covers. These were very effective for a single night, but unfortunately they made the bags wet by condensation, so that they could not be used for a second night without first being dried.

We slept well and kept beautifully warm. It gives you an eerie feeling when you put out your head in the early morning. Everything looks white and unreal and cheerless after the snugness of your bed. The air always feels damp at first, however hard it may be freezing. Your first thought is that a thaw has set in. Then the cold strikes home, and you pop your head in again.

We laced up our boots with cold and fumbling fingers. Our camp site, seen in the daylight, looked the very last word in desolation. We hurriedly stuffed the bags in our rucksacks, together with a good deal of snow, and made our way towards Crib-y-Ddisgyl.

The blizzard was still blowing as strongly as ever and I got one of my eyes frozen up, and had to break the ice on the lashes before I could open it.

We used the rope over Crib Goch and descended to a very welcome breakfast at Pen-y-Pass.

It was the wind that had made the conditions so severe. On a calm day you can feel quite warm and comfortable in a zero temperature.

You won't normally get such bad conditions in the Alps ; you wouldn't attempt to climb in such a storm. But if you do get caught by bad weather it will be far worse. That is why you must always carry a good reserve of food and clothing.

In the Alps you can often save a lot of time by a bivouac, if there are no high huts in the neighbourhood. I remember one very pleasant night we spent at about 11,000 feet, on the way up the Rimpfischhorn (13,790 feet). We slept on the glacier, near the Allalinpass. With our ice-axes we scooped out a fairly level recess and covered it with soft snow, which very soon froze in hard lumps. I chose the worst position (not purposely) and the other two kept sliding on to me all night. Apparently our levelling had not been very accurate.

It was marvellous to waken up in the crisp, cold Alpine air. The sky was cloudless ; the snow was frozen and crunchy. The silence was immense and impressive.

The wind set our ears tingling, but it died down with the coming of the sun. We traversed the main ridge of our peak and altogether had a glorious day. I remember it especially, because it was my first thirteen-thousander.

One more camping adventure — not a true bivouac. It was in the Himalaya, in 1933. The expedition was almost over; we were preparing for the homeward trek. We had run short of food. We had any amount of dried fruit, but no meat and no fresh food of any kind. I need a good deal of meat and was feeling the lack of it very badly.

We were at the Base Camp (14,000 feet) and I

was to go up alone to the Advanced Base (15,200 feet) to bring down as much of the equipment as I could carry ; the remainder had to be left.

The Advanced Base had been established nearly a month ; probably no human being had ever been there before.

I think that the best thing for me to do is to give you an extract from my diary, word for word, as it was written on the Gangotri Glacier, above the source of the holy River Ganges.

Tuesday, 27th June. It was sunny early on, but it began to rain about 10 a.m. and continued off and on throughout the day. There was a mist on the glacier. I wrote letters and re-wrote an article.

I haven't been feeling well for days. In my present state I can't digest Teddie's bakeries, and as there is scarcely anything else and I have lost all appetite for food I am practically starving. To-morrow I am to go up the glacier to evacuate the Advanced Base Camp. I am shivering to-night. I went to bed without supper.

Wednesday, 28th June. Up 7.45. Off 9 a.m. I felt terribly weak and thought of turning back several times, but went on. There was intermittent rain and the sunshine in between was much more intense than it had been before the monsoon, more like the lower valleys.

It soon became evident that I should not get back to the Base Camp the same day ; I was going so slowly. I suffered from gnawing pains in the stomach and a throbbing headache, and had to rest every twenty minutes. A terrible business.

I reached the Advanced Base at 4 p.m.—seven hours for seven miles, and I usually do it in three.

I filled three old tins with water and shut myself in the tent, to keep in the warm air. I had pemmican, Marmite, Ovaltine, and rum punch (with Kendal Mint Cake for sugar). Then I wrapped puttees round my feet, put the sorbo mattress underneath my outer clothes, donned gloves and balaclava, and prepared to spend the night. I had brought no sleeping-bag, as I had meant to return the same day.

It began to get cold at 9.30 p.m. and at 11 o'clock I had a brew of Ovaltine to warm me up. Luckily there are several cookers here.

Thursday, 29th June. I had some more Ovaltine at 2 a.m. I got rather chilly in between boilings, though I had three candles lit to keep me warm. I probably got about two hours' sleep altogether.

It poured in torrents most of the night and the tent leaked. It changed to snow about 5 a.m. At 6 a.m. I had breakfast of lemonade and three ginger nuts, with butter, jam, and Marmite. I couldn't face any more mint cake.

I waited for the snow to clear, but in vain ; so I packed all the most important things in my sack and finally set off at 8.30, leaving the tent desolately standing.

I felt no better than yesterday—very feeble. The snow changed to rain at 9.30 and then stopped, but there were frequent showers all the way. I was so weak that I thought I should never get back. It was exactly like the feeling of starvation, which is what it must be. I had a long search for the Base and almost wept with relief when I saw it at last. I got in at 2.40 p.m.—only six hours to-day.

These have been almost the worst two days of the expedition—nothing really worth suffering for. When I am sitting down I feel quite all right. I felt better after a fair meal of pemmican. What I need is some fresh meat.

Chapter X

ACCIDENTS

THIS is a morbid subject to choose. It is also, perhaps, the aspect of climbing which makes the most interesting reading.

I am not trying, specially, to interest or to depress you. I just want to show you how you can avoid having any mishaps yourself.

It should be impossible, on British rock-climbs, for any one but the leader to get hurt. If you hear about a whole party falling off, you may be sure that they weren't making correct use of belays. And if the leader falls off—well, it's almost always his own fault.

One Good Friday I was leading the very severe Great Central Route on Dow Crags. My second, Alan Hargreaves, was belayed on a small stance, about 30 feet below the ledge known as the Bandstand. Above me was the overhanging " South America Crack."

The crack was terribly strenuous, and near the top the holds seemed to give out completely. My only support was my left arm jammed in the crack; I hung outwards from it and clawed at the rock with the other hand. I made a bad mistake here;

if I had looked around I should have seen a good handhold up on the right.

I squirmed up again until my head came against the overhang ; my balaclava helmet dropped noise-lessly to the bottom. I slipped down again and hung there exhausted. I was dimly conscious of a watching crowd of climbers, away on the left. There were good holds below me ; I could still have descended. But I was too tired to think. I had to go on struggling—for ever and ever, it seemed.

I jerked myself up again in a last despairing effort. I was so done that I could hardly see. Everything went black.

The next thing I knew I was 30 feet lower down, hurtling head-first through the air. My arm had slipped out and I had fallen backwards. I passed about 4 feet outside Alan's stance.

All fear disappeared as soon as I started falling. The struggle had been ghastly, but now it was all out of my hands ; nothing I could do would make any difference. Now I'm in for a nasty smash, I thought ; I knew I might be killed. All I could do was to wait and see what happened. Strangely enough it did not seem to concern me at all. My interest was quite detached. Somebody was crash-ing down to earth, but somehow it seemed to have nothing to do with me.

I fell 70 feet. The first thing I hit was 50 feet below. I can still remember every detail. The rock rushed up and flung me out into the air again.

The rope tightened and jerked me head uppermost, then ran out again and I continued on my downward way.

I landed on the scree at the bottom, with my hips wedged in Hopkinson's Crack. I was conscious of no pain until I stopped ; then my hips hurt fiercely for a few moments, and I thought something must be broken. But I could move, and I soon found that I could walk. I seemed to be uninjured. I climbed straight up to A. B. H., so that I should not lose my nerve.

The only injury was a broken toe. I limped down to Coniston and managed to climb for the remainder of the holiday, though I could not use the outside of my right foot. The toe went yellow and swollen, and each night I took great surgical interest in trying to set it with sticking-plaster.

It was over a year before I dared to attempt G.C.R. again. This time I found the crucial hold, and the crack went quite easily. I even managed to lead the wall above the Bandstand without a shoulder, which had not often been done. So I had my revenge.

Another adventure was on the Javelin Buttress, which forms part of the steep wall at the top of Idwal Slabs. A. B. H. was again my second. This time he had no stance at all, but was suspended from the " Javelin," a curious flake of rock that looks as though it had been stuck on as an after-thought.

The main difficulty of the climb is a mantelshelf,

a few feet higher up. I made one attempt, but the rocks were a little greasy and my rubbers weren't gripping very well, so I came down again. I was standing on a small hold, close to the rock, and to get a better view I leant back a little. To do this I held on to a vertical edge of rock on the right, just as you might grasp the rail before jumping off a bus.

Slowly I felt myself swinging out to the right. There was no left handhold to stop me, and I realized that at the end of the swing I would just fly off into space. I shouted out, "Have you got me?" and jumped for a large ledge 40 feet below on the right. However, the rope swung me round, and I found myself suspended on the steep slab below the belay. I had fallen 15 or 20 feet, and Alan had not let the rope run out an inch.

Not the slightest damage was done to either of us. Even Alan's hands were unhurt. On the Dow Crag incident they had been burnt and torn almost to the bone.

I was quite unshaken ; I took off my rubbers and finished the climb in stockinged-feet, which grip much better on damp rock.

Now A. B. H. is about a couple of stones lighter than I am, and yet he managed to hold me. That was because he was correctly belayed. A belay to him is an engineering problem, not to be used until it is as perfect as possible. He delights in constructing safe anchorages in the most appalling situations.

This fall was, of course, due entirely to gross carelessness on my part. I had suddenly found myself able to do the hardest climbs and had grown over-confident. I had had a number of falls without serious injury and had begun to be less frightened of accidents. That is to say, I was willing to take risks ; I thought boldness a better policy than discretion. That is a most dangerous state of mind, and one that is very common among young climbers between the ages of nineteen and twenty-one ; that is why such a lot of accidents occur amongst university students.

Loose rock causes a few accidents, but stones seldom fall by themselves on our mountains. A friend of mine was climbing Faith, on the Slabs, a short time ago. He was about 30 feet up when a large stone shot down the rocks and hit him in the middle of the forehead. He knew nothing about it until he found himself lying at the bottom, with an anxious crowd around him. His skull was fractured, but a little thing like that didn't worry Bill ; he walked down to the road. He still has a neat little dinge in the centre of his forehead.

Some one had knocked down the stone, of course ; I believe it was a lady climber—a beginner, on her first day on the rocks. So see that you don't do anything like that. And whatever you do, never roll stones down a cliff, where there may be people climbing, or sheep about.

On Easter Sunday, 1936, I was on Ben Nevis. Four of us had been camping by the windswept little lochan, half-way up. The snow was plentiful and very hard—almost as hard as ice.

We were on our way up to the Tower Gap Chimney, where we were expecting to have some good sport with hard ice. We came to a great crevasse, where the snow had shrunk away from the cliff; it was nearly 100 feet deep and in the Alps would have been called a bergschrund.

Then we had a 40-foot pitch of steep ice, which took some time. The snow slope above was fairly steep and very hard; several blows of the axe were needed for each step. We were climbing on two separate ropes; Derrick and I were on the first, and Alfred and Dorothy were on the other. I was leading and cutting the steps; then we changed places, and Derrick took over the lead.

We were ascending a kind of scoop. On the right were steep iced rocks; an overhanging line of dark crag rose above us on the left. Our snow-slope was about 30 feet wide.

Suddenly there was a great clattering, far above us. It grew louder, but sounded well away to the right. Then small stones began to whiz over the edge of the cliff on the left. This was just the beginning. Have you ever watched a cart-load of bricks being emptied? That is what it looked like. A great avalanche of stones crashed over the rocks, just above our heads. They came in an endless stream. They rumbled and sang past our ears, and split in fragments all around. It was terrifying to see them dropping thickly out of the sky. The slope above us became a heaving mass of grating rocks.

I think Alfred was the first to be hit. A large rock broke his arm, which he had put up to protect his head. He went down, but Dorothy held him. Then she too was hit and they were both swept down.

I tried desperately to reach the little crevasse on the left. There was shelter there, and I should be able to hold Derrick. I attempted to dig the pick of my axe into the hard snow ; there was certainly no time for step-cutting. It was all in vain ; I was swept down by the shooting stream of rocks.

I went head-first ; it seems to be a habit of mine. I could see my camera going down in front. It was an easy winner ; I never saw it again. Then I went over the 40-foot ice-wall and landed with a sickening jolt on the edge of the crevasse. Derrick must have arrived soon afterwards to complete the party. He went plonk into a hole, so that only his head and shoulders were visible. He looked rather funny. Alfred was a few feet down the slope, held by the rope. Dorothy was close to me.

The stones continued for another 500 feet. I cannot imagine why we didn't do likewise.

Alfred was the most cheerful of the party, although he had a broken arm and a gash that ran half-way up his face. He also had a bone broken on his ankle. He sat and smoked cigarette after cigarette. Derrick had concussion and looked grey and drawn. His hands were mangled. Dorothy had her face and one leg badly cut and various muscles strained. I had a shoulder torn so that one arm was useless. My ribs were damaged. I could not breathe sitting down and felt sick standing up. After a time the faintness disappeared and I felt quite comfortable.

We had all lost our axes, so we could not help ourselves at all. It was very chilly sitting there on the snow, waiting. At intervals we shouted for help.

Our shouts were heard by Hemming and McCallum of the Scottish Mountaineering Club, who climbed up to our rescue. We owe a lot to them ; they were most skilful and efficient. They retrieved our axes ; mine was broken in two.

The first thing was to get Derrick down. He was lowered on his back down the slope, his arms sticking out pathetically in front. I couldn't help being amused ; he looked so ridiculous, although he was in a bad enough way, poor chap.

The procedure was for one or other of the rescue party to carve a great platform out of the snow every hundred feet. Then the whole party would be assembled there. I managed to descend on my own, cutting steps with my uninjured arm and the broken ice-axe.

The accident had happened at two o'clock. It was seven before we reached the hut, about 800 feet lower down. Without help we could never have managed it at all. It was really a miracle that none of us was killed, since we had fallen over 250 feet, apart from the bombardment we had suffered.

I made my way back to the tent, where I was

looked after by my friend Bob Frost, who was camping near by. The other three were taken to hospital.

I had a poor night. I could not lie on my left side on account of my ribs, nor on my right because of my shoulder; so I had to try and sleep on my back. I gave up the attempt when it grew light, and read through the Ben Nevis guide from cover to cover.

I left the other three in hospital and was back at work in Liverpool on the Tuesday.

This accident was pure bad luck. We could not possibly have foreseen it. It was freezing quite hard, so there was no reason for us to expect an avalanche. Whether the stones were loosened by the sun, or whether some one knocked them down, we were never able to discover.

None of these accidents had very serious results, but you can see how easily they might have had. Most of them happened when I was in my 'teens, when I certainly was inclined to take more risks than I should have done.

A fatal accident is a very terrible thing. Don't think of yourself, but think of the effect on all your relations and friends if anything were to happen to you. Or think how you would feel if you had to meet the parents of a friend who had been killed while climbing with you.

I don't want to put you off; there is no need for any of these things to happen to you. It all depends on yourself. So be careful; then your climbing will bring you nothing but pleasure.

CHAPTER XI

ALPINE CLIMBING

THERE is nothing to compare with the thrill of your first visit to the Alps, especially if you have never been abroad before. Even the Customs seem exciting—but only the first time. Then there is the Channel crossing and the interest of finding out whether you are a good sailor. I overheard one old tar saying to an oldish lady—she must have come from Ireland, because her face was green: "Why, Mum! if it wasn't for seasickness there wouldn't be any fun in a sailor's life."

Dieppe just before dawn—a ghostly fairy harbour in the pale half-light. The boat-train by the water's edge; the French porters; the sleepy shuffle through the Customs. It is all the more wonderful because it is the prelude to the long-dreamed-of Alps. Then Paris—and the endless train journey—until you get your first view of the Alps.

They look small at first, these Alps, but it is marvellous to be seeing the snows at last, hot and sticky as you are in the stuffy carriage. Bigger and bigger they grow, for many hours, until finally you are actually in the midst of them.

I advise you to sail by night and have the train journey in the daytime. A night in the train may put you out of sorts for a couple of days. Also, there is so much to be seen. If you have the time and money to split your journey, so much the better. Personally I have always grudged spending a single unnecessary hour of my precious fortnight away from the mountains.

Don't believe any grim tales you may hear about the French third class carriages. They do not compare with the English ones, but they are not at all bad.

A knowledge of French or German is useful but by no means essential. English is spoken at most of the popular centres, and everyone is very understanding and anxious to help. A Swiss waitress displayed no surprise when, instead of ordering two eggs for breakfast, I ordered two cows. She must have thought that I was carrying the Englishman's well-known love of roast beef rather to excess.

If you can spare the time you will do well to spend the first few days in doing long training walks. I have never been able to do this and consequently have usually been miserably sick and ill at 12,000 feet on my first day out.

For your first climb choose something fairly easy between 10,000 and 11,000 feet. You aren't likely to be mountain-sick at this height; in fact some people can go straight up to 13,000 or 14,000 feet without turning a hair.

The first thing to do is to buy provisions for a couple of days. You must be prepared to live very simply in the hut, since you don't want to waste a lot of time with cooking. Eggs, bread-and-butter, and tea are all you need for breakfast. For the evening meal some kind of soup is best, since it can all be prepared in the same pan. Two or three packets of soup, a couple of eggs, and a tin of corned beef, all mixed up together, will make a sustaining spread for three. This doesn't sound very appetizing, but it will seem like a royal banquet after a hard day's climbing.

Each egg should be wrapped up separately in newspaper and packed in a strong box. You will find that the local shopkeepers are quite used to doing this.

For the actual climbing you should take some bread, a lot of chocolate, some boiled sweets, and some tinned meat or fish (sardines go down very well). An aluminium water-bottle is a necessity, and a small flask of brandy should also be carried. Fruit is very welcome, but it should be something that is easily carried ; oranges are probably best.

You must not think that you can learn to be an Alpinist merely by following what I have to tell you. You can learn only by experience, and nobody knows all there is to know. All I can do is to give you a few impressions and one or two useful hints. This is really no disadvantage, since you must start off with an experienced party. You should have at

least a couple of seasons' practice before you lead
your own party.

You set off for the hut soon after lunch. It is
very hot and your rucksack weighs well over
30 pounds. You are wearing shorts and shirt and
carrying most of your climbing-clothes on your
back. The path goes up through a steep wood,
and you grow more and more hot and sticky.

You keep going, slowly and steadily, and after
two hours you rise above the tree-line and come
out on to a grassy alp, bright with flowers. You
stop at a cowshed and have a drink of milk. Some
people say you shouldn't do this, because when you
are hot the milk turns to cheese and rattles about
in lumps inside you. A nasty prospect—but as
long as it doesn't turn to gorgonzola I'm willing
to risk it.

The ground is less steep here, and the air is
cooler. The path winds pleasantly among boulders
and across streams in a way that reminds you of
home. But great snow peaks rise all round, and
the hot Alpine sun is burning down on you. You
put on your hat—a white sun-hat is as good as
anything, though stained and battered trilbys seem
to lead the fashion.

You gain the top of a grassy spur and look down
on to your first glacier. It pushes its snout of dirty
ice right down into the trees. It isn't as white as
you had expected, except higher up where it is
covered with snow. The lower part is broken into
a wild jumbled mass.

At last you see the hut a few hundred feet above. The path zigzags up a steep and stony slope, and it takes you another fifteen minutes to reach the door. The ascent has taken four and a half hours and you are over 9,000 feet above sea-level. You find it hard to realize—three times as high as Scafell or Tryfan and yet only at the foot of the climbing.

The hut is built of wood and perched on the very crest of the ridge. A great jagged cliff drops straight down to the glacier from the back window. No place for sleep-walking, you think. The view is superb—nothing but mountains. The whole world is rock and snow ; the valleys are just deep dark holes—they don't really seem to matter.

You go inside. It is dark after the sunlight, and at first you can hardly see. Then you make out a long wooden table and a few rough chairs. There is one other party there and they are going to bed. But they have lit the stove and got some water, thank goodness !

You make your tea and soup and then go to the door for a last look at the view. There is a chilly wind and the sun has disappeared. The valleys are in shadow and the snow looks dead and cold.

You go up to bed. You feel a little breathless going upstairs, but that is all you notice of the height. You take off your boots, put on your climbing-clothes ready for the morning and all lie down side by side on the straw mattress. The other party is sleeping soundly, so one of you quietly opens a window. Continentals aren't fond of fresh air.

There are lots of blankets and you feel quite warm. But it is strange being in bed at nine o'clock, and besides you are too excited to sleep. The noisy arrival of another party does not help matters.

" It's a lovely morning ; get up, you lazy brute." You almost wish it was raining ; you feel sure you've only been in bed ten minutes. " Come on ; it's one o'clock." Off come the blankets, and you are hauled on to the floor. Beastly hearty blighter !

You sleepily pull on your boots with cold fingers. The candles make weird flickering shadows of the rucksacks on the table. You eat a silent, gloomy breakfast of boiled eggs and tea and hunks of bread. The two lanterns are lit and you set off at two o'clock. There is not a cloud in the sky and millions of stars are gleaming coldly down.

You get on to the moraine, a ridge of stones of all sizes, from great boulders to dust, that have been carried down by the glacier. They slip and slide under your feet, and you bang your shins. The lantern is always shining in the wrong place. How you long for your warm bed ! Surely nothing can make this nightmare worth while !

At last there are glimmers of daylight. The lanterns are put out. Suddenly a snowy summit turns blood-red, then golden. In a few minutes all the mountains are dazzling in the sunshine.

At last you reach a sunlit patch of snow. All

148

your tiredness disappears ; you feel glad to be alive. You sit down and have your second breakfast, basking in the warm sunshine.

Half an hour on snow in an Alpine sun will burn all the skin off your face, unless you take suitable precautions. So you must now cover it thickly with a red greasy substance. There are several brands—Sèchehaye or Antilux are both excellent. Ordinary grease is no use ; you must have the colour to cut out the rays that do the damage. It is hard to keep the lips covered ; a good tip is to risk being thought " pansy " and use lipstick. After a few days your skin will get sunburnt and you will find that you need very little protection.

You must also put on your snow-goggles. As with sunburn, you don't feel the effects of snowblindness until the damage is done. You may feel quite comfortable all day and then, in the evening, have violent pain in the eyes and a splitting headache, which may last for a day or two. You may even go completely blind. Luckily there is rarely any permanent damage, but you may easily have half your holiday ruined.

Now you descend to the glacier, which you have to cross to reach your peak on the other side. The glacier is snow-covered and smooth, and looks very simple. You rope up on the edge. You take the middle place on the rope. You keep about 15 feet apart and you have the unpleasant job of carrying two sets of coils, one for the leader and one for

No. 3. There are crevasses on either side, but the way you are going seems quite free. You have to be careful not to let the rope trail on the snow and not to let it drag on either of your companions.

You are walking happily along, admiring the scenery, when suddenly your foot goes through the snow. Your watchful friends immediately tighten the rope and you draw back with a nasty start. You look down into a green hole, which opens into an icy cavern of unknown depth. After this adventure you proceed very, very cautiously.

You observe the crevasses on either side and see that many of them run right across the glacier. You can follow roughly their line by a series of holes, or else by a slight depression in the snow. As soon as the leader comes to a doubtful stretch he probes in the snow with the shaft of his axe. If he reaches hard ice, he knows that all is well. But if the axe goes right in, then it is over a crevasse. So he must probe again until he finds ice. Then he knows he is on the solid glacier, or else on an ice bridge. He is very careful to place his feet exactly where his axe has been. And you, in your turn, must follow exactly in his footsteps.

If your companion falls into a crevasse you must immediately plunge your axe into the snow as a belay and hold him tightly. It is often a difficult job to pull him out, since the rope bites into the snow and jams. In extreme cases you can tie one rope to the belayed axe. He can then climb up

A CREVASSE.

This is quite safe, as it is clearly visible. It would be dangerous if hidden under a covering of snow.

this rope while the two above ground haul him up by the other.

It is obvious that you must always proceed at right-angles to the general line of crevasses, not parallel with them. Otherwise the whole party may be over a crevasse at the same time. This is where an experienced leader is so essential. He can judge which way the crevasses run, even though he cannot see them.

I once fell into a crevasse. It was dark too—eleven o'clock at night. I was wearing the rope round my neck.

That may sound rather a curious thing to do, but this is how it happened. We were climbing the Zinal Rothorn by the South Ridge—a very long and difficult rock-climb. It was the first day of the holiday and we were very slow. One of the party would persist in going to sleep. I would keep on being sick.

We had to run out the full 100 feet of rope on the rocks. It was just getting dark when we started descending from 13,000 feet. There was no time to be lost, so I just coiled the surplus rope round my shoulders until it was short enough for the easier work below. Then followed exhausting hours of soft snow and confusing route-finding. I was absolutely worn out. We were descending a steep glacier slope. It was very dark, though lightning was flickering about the great peaks of the Mischabel, on the other side of the Zermatt Valley. Instead of probing for every step I was merely driving in my axe and striding past it. I was very tired.

I stepped on to thin air. The rope tightened, slipped off my shoulders and wound itself round my neck. I was rapidly getting strangled and had to tell Marco to slacken off. My axe was driven firmly into the snow above and I hung grimly on to it, with my feet swinging about in space. By a great effort I managed to get one foot on to the other side of the crevasse, which was luckily at a much lower level. It was a nasty moment. It was all my own fault, of course. If I had taken the trouble to re-tie and had used proper methods on the descent I should have been perfectly safe. That is the danger of getting over-tired ; carelessness almost always creeps in.

Now to return to your expedition. You find the way barred by a large open crevasse. There is no danger of dropping in unawares ; you can see the great ugly-looking rift stretching away into the distance on either side. It is too wide to jump ; the only possibility is a rickety-looking snow-bridge. The leader goes cautiously across, whilst you stand belayed, ready to pull him back if the bridge collapses. When your turn comes you are held from both sides. You look down the shiny blue-green walls of ice, which disappear into the blackness hundreds of feet below.

You find that the glacier is separated from the rock of your peak by a bergschrund—a special kind of crevasse that is caused by the ice slipping away from a higher slope or, as in this case, shrinking away from rock. Ordinary crevasses are formed by pressure. It doesn't really matter into which kind you happen to fall.

It is necessary to descend into the bergschrund, so you put on your crampons. These are spikes, about an inch and a half in length, on a frame which is attached to the boot by webbing straps (see Illustration, page 79). Like the ice-axe, goggles and snow-cream (but not the rope), these may be conveniently purchased abroad. Get a pair with ten spikes.

The leader climbs down into the bergschrund, cutting small steps. You hold his rope carefully while he crosses a flimsy ice-bridge and climbs up the rocks on the other side, until he reaches a rock-belay. Then you cautiously descend. You press each foot hard and clean into the ice and find that the crampons give an amazing grip. On the rocks you find them very awkward, however.

Now you have to cross a couloir—a wide gully. It is filled with hard snow, so you keep on your crampons. There is no need to cut steps here ; you can walk quite easily in your crampons. They give you a wonderful feeling of confidence.

There is a deep dirty groove running down the centre of the couloir. " Falling stones," says the leader ; " in a couple of hours the place will be alive with them." So there was some point in the early start, after all.

You all sit down and eat some chocolate and an orange. The aluminium water-bottle is re-filled from a little trickle of melting ice. You take off your crampons and start up the rocks leading to the ridge. This time you fasten your crampons on the outside of your rucksack. You had them inside before, and all your spare clothes are covered with orange-juice.

The rocks are easy, but very delightful—lovely red granite. You all move together, carrying coils. It is difficult to prevent the rope from catching on the rough rock. You don't use belays—just watch carefully and look out for suitable belays to use in case of an emergency. You realize that each member of the party must share the responsibility. Even the most expert leader cannot get a party of clumsy novices safely up an Alpine climb, as on a homeland route. It is true that the guides manage to do this ; but then they seem to develop a flair for looking after their charges.

No. 3 has now taken over the leadership, and the former leader takes his place on the lower end of the rope. Leading is a strain, and it is a great help if it can be shared.

Now and again, on difficult bits, you use belays as in English climbing, but most of the time you all move together.

You come to a slope of fairly hard snow, where you can kick steps. " How would you like this if you were sinking in up to your knees ? " says one of your companions. " That's what it'll be like when the sun gets on it." Another reason for starting early.

Your head suddenly comes dramatically over the crest of the ridge and you look down the other side. The cliff drops down in a breathtaking wall of sunlit rock, plastered with ice. You have never even imagined such dizzy sheerness—thousands of feet of it.

The ridge is more wonderful than you had ever dreamed it could be. It is very narrow and the rock is bright pink, and everything is brilliant and thrilling. You feel a hero, tremendously alive and strong. You wish it could all go on for ever.

Sometimes the way is barred by fantastic pinnacles; these are known as gendarmes. Some you climb over; others you must go round. None of the climbing is really difficult; you have done much harder pitches in Wales. But this is the real thing. There is such a lot of it; everything is on such a terrific scale. You can't just walk round and find an easier way. Already you begin to think of the Welsh climbs as mere boulder-problems—difficult enough, but not very important.

The whole art of Alpine climbing is different. You must move quickly and yet safely; you must not waste time; you must be familiar with snow and ice, be good at route-finding, be an efficient organizer.

A little more easy scrambling, and you are on your first Alpine summit—too proud and happy for words. It is only nine o'clock, yet it seems ages since you left the hut. You just sit and drink in the view. You have lived for this moment.

All the well-known Alpine giants, about which you have read so longingly, are grouped around. The sun is very hot, and you spend the happiest hour of your life basking on the burning rocks.

You descend by an easier route. Sometimes you have to face inwards, but usually you can face out, or else go down sideways, with one steadying hand on the rocks.

" Why not go down that nice little snow-slope ? " you say.

" See those lumps of snow at the bottom ? " replies your friend. " That's avalanche débris. Your nice little snow-slope is the rubbish-chute for half the mountain."

At last you are running with great strides down a slope of soft wet snow. Crossing the glacier has no terrors for you now, and you are soon at the hut again. It is cool and pleasant inside, and you make some tea. Your face is red and burning.

By two o'clock in the afternoon you are down in the valley once more. You feel you have earned the delicious French pastries you get at tea-time. You have your tea at a table set among the trees, listening to the band and feeling thoroughly contented and pleased with life.

CHAPTER XII

THUNDERSTORMS ON THE CHARDONNET

YOU are probably quite fed-up with being told what to do and what not to do. As a matter of fact I am rather fed-up with telling you. You will learn a lot more, I expect, if I recount some of my adventures ; you will note the mistakes I made and see what punishment I received for making them.

Most of my expeditions would not make good stories ; it is only when things go wrong that there is anything to talk about. So I will tell you about an exciting ascent of the Aiguille du Chardonnet (12,557 feet).

I was staying at the Refuge d'Argentière with my friend Bob Frost. It was his first Alpine season, but he was already a brilliant rock-climber. The previous day we had traversed the Aiguille d'Argentière (12,824 feet), Bob's first Alpine peak. There had been a violent storm in the evening, so we were not very hopeful about the weather.

We started out from the hut at 4 a.m. The sky was heavy with threatening clouds. It should be quite cloudless at this hour of the morning, so we knew the weather was very doubtful. However, we decided to go on until it got definitely bad ; we had climbed a lot together and could trust each other implicitly.

We ascended the Glacier du Chardonnet until we were near the col. Our peak was on the left, but we did not know where to start the ascent. Our guide-book (all in French) told us to make for a rib running up to the left of the summit. But we could see about ten spiky pinnacles, any one of which might have been the summit. So we just had to guess—and we guessed wrongly.

We crossed the bergschrund by a tongue of avalanche débris, which was safe enough, of course, at this early hour. For a time all went well. We had some easy scrambling, and then some interesting rock-climbing of moderate difficulty. To save time we climbed unroped ; we could trust ourselves on the rocks.

We climbed a snow-ridge until we came to some impossible rocks. Then we worked up to the right, but could get no farther. So down we came again. Then we ascended a steep gully, which steadily grew more and more difficult. A little higher up we saw a ledge leading out to the left, and hopefully followed it. The same thing happened again ; we got some way up the rocks and then had to descend.

We continued up the gully, which was now vertical and very difficult. All the rocks were covered with new snow. There was one really severe pitch, which Bob climbed without a pause.

158

I managed to get up, but didn't enjoy it and suggested that it was high time we used the rope.

The gully got quite impossible, and we were forced out to the right. Here we were well and truly stuck. All the surrounding rocks were un-climbable—above and below and on either side. To add to our troubles it was starting to snow quite heavily. We had no doubt by this time that we were off the proper route.

Away on the right was a wide snow-couloir. There was only one thing for it—a 50-foot abseil. That was a simple enough matter, but it meant that we had burnt our boats; we couldn't get back again.

The couloir would have been easy in decent conditions—but the conditions weren't decent. The slope was formed of a foot of soft snow resting on ice—all ready to avalanche at a touch. This meant that we had to keep to the solid ice on the left, climbing the rocks wherever possible. This was fairly safe, but difficult and very slow. We moved one at a time, leading through. Bob would go up until he could find a rock-belay; it often meant running out 100 feet of rope. Then I would follow, pass him, and proceed to another belay. All the time we were wasting vital hours.

There was easier ground on the other side of the couloir, but we simply dared not cross, even on a rope; the danger of an avalanche was too great.

At last things eased off, and we managed to gain a small subsidiary ridge, quite close to the summit. Possibly we had made a new route. The weather had suddenly changed, and it was now fine and sunny, though there was a chilly wind blowing.

The ridge was delightful. There was one difficult but very enjoyable gendarme of rough red granite and then a short snow-ridge which led to the summit.

It was now 2.20 p.m.—we were over four hours late. The ascent had taken ten hours, instead of five or six. However we thought we were safe at last. The weather looked so promising that we had a well deserved forty-minutes rest on the summit.

When we started the descent we noticed an inky-black cloud, which completely hid all the country to the west. We were going down the north-west ridge, which was very much easier than our route up the mountain. There was just one difficult pitch before the col, which we had nearly reached when the storm broke upon us. A sudden gale had sprung up, it was snowing and hailing, and the lightning was flashing all around. The thunder was deafening ; it ripped through the clouds and seemed as though it would burst our ear-drums. It was a terrifying experience. You are very likely to be struck by the lightning when you are on the crest of an Alpine ridge. We cowered down in the snow, so as to make less of a mark.

When the lightning seemed to have retreated a little we made a move. There were some snow-covered crevasses to be crossed ; it was hard to be careful with the driving hail lashing our faces.

THE SUMMIT OF THE CHARDONNET (12,557 feet).
Just before the thunderstorms started.

A MODERN ALPINE HUT.
The Refuge du Couvercle (8,851 feet), near Chamonix. Mont
Blanc is seen behind.

We reached the col at last, just as another storm was upon us. We now had to descend the face on the left, but we didn't know where to start. The guide-book described only the ascent. It told you to " oblique to the right," but did not say whereabouts on the ridge this would land you. No doubt it would be perfectly obvious when you were going up.

We started down a little gully. What happened below we could not tell ; all we could see was darkly swirling cloud. It was hailing viciously and the rocks were covered with ice. In forty minutes we had descended only 200 feet. The cloud thinned for an instant and we could see that the slope below steepened and curved out of sight. It was nearly five o'clock. A horrible feeling of hopelessness descended upon me. I glanced at Bob to see how he was standing the strain. He looked anxious, but showed no signs of collapse.

We climbed up to the col again. I decided that the only chance was to cross the next peak, the Aiguille Adams Reilly. The route from the col on the other side appeared to be down a straightforward couloir, which we thought we should be able to find, even in the cloud.

The aiguille was quite easy, but it was a different tale on the other side. It was early in the season— the beginning of July—and a bad season at that ; and the ice of the glacier reached high up the rocks. We saw the line of nailmarks descending beneath the ice. We had to traverse high up, across snow-covered rocks and bits of ice. Luckily there was a lull in the storm, but we were losing more and more time, having to move singly all the way.

We came to a 15-foot slab, covered thinly with ice. After a great deal of difficulty I managed to fix myself on to a very sketchy belay. There was no hold for my feet; I was just hanging there. I lowered Bob down the slab, told him to plant himself as firmly as possible, and jumped down. He fielded me neatly. The snow I kicked down started several small avalanches on the steep snow-covered ice below.

We reached the Col Adams Reilly (11,040 feet) at seven o'clock—only two hours of daylight left.

We found the couloir easily and made a quick descent. The snow was soft but we could get good ice-axe belays. At last we were able to move together once more. Avalanches were falling all round, but we kept clear of the deep groove in the middle of the couloir and felt safe enough.

There was another thunderstorm and more thick cloud, but we were past worrying. We were at least going downhill.

There was a bergschrund and a steep 20-foot snow wall at the bottom, followed by some difficult rocks, but after that all danger was over. We reached the main Argentière Glacier at nine o'clock, just as it was getting dark. What a sigh of relief we breathed ! If either of us had been overcome by exhaustion, or if the nerve-strain had been too much, there would have been very little hope of coming through alive. It wouldn't have helped much if we had lasted out the night, since it snowed solidly for the next two days.

The danger was over, but we still had more troubles to come. There was another violent thunderstorm and a thick cloud descended on to the glacier. It was pitch dark and raining in torrents. We knew the hut was a few hundred feet up the slope on the left, but whether we had passed it or not we could not tell. We just stumbled on, in dazed exhaustion. We were quite resigned to spending the night out on the glacier. It would have been unpleasant, but not serious at this altitude. I had a torch, but I switched it on only now and again, to save the battery.

We were wet to the skin, but so tired that we would have been glad to sleep anywhere. I shone the torch again—surely those were tracks in the snow !

Fifteen minutes later we were in the hut. It was eleven o'clock ; we had been out nineteen hours. We had half expected a search party, but the guardian was in bed. He didn't care.

We spent most of the next day in bed.

Chapter XIII

A PERFECT ALPINE DAY

IT was ten days later that we reached the Montanvert. We had spent four nights at the Refuge du Couvercle and the weather had been hopeless. The only peak we managed to bag was the Moine (11,198 feet), usually an easy climb. It was snowing heavily, and it took us four hours without a halt to reach the summit, which was covered with two feet of fresh snow. Rock-climbing in such conditions is not a picnic.

We had only two days left, so we decided to descend to Chamonix and make for home, stopping anywhere in France that seemed to offer a chance of sunshine.

When we reached the Montanvert, however, the weather was looking much more hopeful, and the local guides promised a fine day on the morrow.

The Montanvert is a big hotel at about 7,000 feet; after the rough life of the hut we felt that we were really living in luxury. We even managed to persuade them to cook us eggs for our two o'clock breakfast.

We set off at 3 a.m. It was a lovely morning, with a cloudless starlit sky. The path wound beautifully across the hillside, through rocks and flowers. We came round a corner and suddenly saw the lights of Chamonix, 4,000 feet below. We felt as though we were looking down on an enchanted fairy garden.

Then we reached the steep little Nantillons Glacier. We put on our crampons for a 20-foot ice-slope, but did not really need them after that.

We passed some wonderful ice-grottoes, glowing with mysterious lights of blue and green. Their floors were jumbled blocks of ice, half covering dark and sinister-looking cracks, that tunnelled down for hundreds of feet into the frozen heart of the glacier. All around were great pinnacles of ice, waiting to crash down at the first touch of the sun. They looked weird and evil in the grey light of dawn.

If a climber falls into a crevasse it is often impossible for one man to pull him out unaided. To overcome this difficulty we were climbing on a double length of line. If Bob had fallen in I should have belayed the rope and pulled on one length whilst he climbed up the other. We also took extra care and did not once get caught napping.

We were aiming for the Aiguille des Grands Charmoz (11,293 feet). We had wanted to climb the famous Grépon, but it was hopelessly iced and had been done only once that season.

There was a good snow-bridge across the bergschrund, and we were soon kicking steps up the couloir that led to the Charmoz-Grépon Col. The snow was very good and we made rapid progress. Just below the col the snow was soft and deep, and we had to be careful. Some easy rocks and a strenuous little crack landed us on the summit at 7.50 a.m. It had seemed quite an easy climb, and we were well ahead of the guide-book time. But our adventures had not yet begun.

We stayed an hour on the top, eating and lazing. It was hot and sunny, and it was delightful just to lie on the rock and gaze at the scenery. The huge mass of Mont Blanc, towering high above everything else, looked dazzling against the deep blue sky. In front, the dark slender needle of the Grépon provided a striking contrast.

The North-west Ridge of the Grands Charmoz consists of about a dozen spiky pinnacles. We had an idea that there was a regular route over these, right down to the Petit Charmoz. We set off just before nine o'clock.

We crossed two little pinnacles before we came to our first real difficulty. We found ourselves sitting astride an absolute knife-edge, with a vertical 20-foot drop cutting us off from the next section of the ridge. We decided that we had better rope-down.

The next pitch was a difficult crack up the gendarme known as the Bâton Wicks, a curious pinnacle, looking like a church steeple which has had its top lifted off and then put back again, not quite in the right place.

The whole ridge was very sharp and thin. Imagine walking along a garden wall and finding your way blocked every few yards by 50-foot monuments and chimney-stacks and gaping holes. And imagine that your wall is several thousand feet high and made of red granite, and you have the Charmoz. The exposure was really terrific. On the Mer de Glace side the precipice was nearly vertical for close on 4,000 feet. Half-way a great slab of ice, several hundred feet in width, was clinging like plaster to a wall.

The next gendarme gave us a lot of trouble. The only way round was a very smooth slab on the left-hand side. It was my turn to lead—we had been taking alternate pitches—and I didn't like it at all. In the end we threw the rope over the top of the pinnacle, so that I was held from above.

We were now at the bottom of another deep cleft in the ridge. The next pinnacle looked quite unclimbable, and we could see no way round. To the right, away out on the face of the cliff, there seemed to be some nail-marked holds. But how had climbers managed to reach them? There was a holdless overhanging gap between. Then we noticed a belay, and the difficulty was solved. I tied a loop of rope over the belay, grasped it with both hands and swung across, with my legs dangling clear over several thousand feet of jagged dizziness. After all it usually makes no difference whether you fall 100 feet or 1,000 feet; the result is the same. Also, my rope was passed over the belay, so that I was really absolutely safe. All the same, I was glad when I got a footing on the other side.

Then we had another 20-foot abseil from a sharp pinnacle. The bottom overhung. I went down a little to one side, and when I reached the overhang, of course, I could no longer reach the rock with my feet. I got my right hand trapped between the rope and the rock and swung across for 3 feet, with the whole of my weight on the rope scraping my knuckles against the saw-edged granite. The backs of three fingers were quite white afterwards; then they grew red and raw-looking, and started to bleed—but only a little, since they were burnt as well as scraped. It was very clumsy of me, and I must confess that I chuckled audibly when Bob did the same thing, though not so badly, on another abseil.

One more abseil, and we seemed to have reached the end of everything. The ridge dropped in a terrific step of several hundred feet. We had mis-translated a phrase in the guide-book and thought that the route went straight on. We sat down and had a discussion.

There was a belay with an old loop round it, so we weren't the first here. That decided us. Bob took a loop of line out of his rucksack and started to abseil. As soon as he had started I noticed what an ancient and moth-eaten loop he was using. A voice from the depths assured me that it was all right, but I thought it safer to hang on to his rope with one hand as well; I was hanging on to the rock with the other.

Thirty feet—still no belay. Forty feet, fifty feet

—he was getting near the end of the rope ; he could abseil no more than sixty feet on the doubled 120-foot line.

At 60 feet Bob reached a ledge—but no belay. I told him to tie on, and held his rope, so that he could go another 60 feet if necessary on a single rope. After wandering about for some time he shouted up that he could see something that looked like a belay about 50 feet to his left ; he thought it would be possible to reach it. But what then ? We should have had to abseil again, and if then we couldn't reach another belay we should be completely stuck.

I felt sure this must be the way, and decided to risk it. I turned the loop round, so that the wear should come on a fresh spot. I think it was the sight of that worn piece of line that made me pause. If I went down and pulled the rope after me, there was no chance of return. I thought of the two of us, on that ledge below, without a belay. Suppose we could not reach the next belay. I had a vision of one of us slipping—then a dreadful pause—then the jerk of the rope, whipping the other off into space. Or waiting through the freezing night for help that might never come. Bad weather ; exhaustion and frostbite ; a last despairing effort— hanging on until all strength had gone ; then crashing down. No !

" Come up, you fool ! " I shouted to Bob. He had been down over half an hour. I had to pull him up more than half of the 60 feet. I still shudder when I think how near I was to such an act of madness.

So now we had to go back the same way. It was just noon. We had made three abseils ; how were we going to get up them again ?

We managed to avoid the first abseil by working across the face on the right and up a crack. Then we came to the place where I had skinned my hand. This was a tough nut to crack. By standing on Bob's shoulders—painful with tricounis—I could reach the top of the overhang. But the slab above seemed to be quite holdless. The sharp edge of it wasn't more than a couple of feet away ; if only I could reach it ! I tried to hook my ice-axe over, but it wouldn't hold. Then Bob had a try, on my shoulders. No luck ! Then I stood on my axe, held against the rock by Bob, but that was more hopeless than the shoulder. We explored on all sides, but could find no way round. We began to grow a little anxious.

Then I remembered my early adventure in the Javelin Gully, and decided to try some more cowboy stuff. At the second attempt I managed to throw a loop of rope over the top of the pinnacle. The rest was simple, though strenuous. I pulled the rope on one side of the pinnacle, and Bob came up on the other. Then he pulled me up bodily.

Bob led across the delicate slab that had bothered me so much, and did not seem to find it very hard. It was also his turn to lead when we came to the next pinnacle we had abseiled. This was very

R. C. FROST ON THE RIDGE OF THE CHARMOZ.

hard; I found it most difficult just following up.

We were back on the summit again at 1.40 p.m., after five hours of severe climbing. Our arms and fingers were beginning to feel rather tired. We looked down and saw two figures at the foot of the couloir. They had started out about half an hour later than we had; we had seen their lanterns behind us.

The couloir was very soft and slushy, but safe enough except at the top, where we went with care and used rock-belays.

On the glacier a kindly French party gave us some tea they had made on a spirit stove. They laughed when I rushed forward so eagerly that I put my foot through a crevasse.

It was delightful strolling down the lovely path. It was all so safe and friendly; we felt pleasantly tired and thoroughly happy and contented. We reached the Montanvert at half-past five, had tea and got down to Chamonix before eight.

We sat in a steaming bath and shaved off a week's growth of beard. Two days later we were in London. It had been a most glorious holiday, in spite of the weather.

People often find it hard to get on together through all the difficulties and discomforts of an Alpine holiday, but in Bob Frost I had found the perfect companion. We planned to do great things together. But fate willed otherwise. Tragically he was killed the following year in a motor-cycle accident.

CHAPTER XIV

OFF TO THE HIMALAYA

HOW would you feel if you got the chance to visit the greatest mountain range in the world—the Himalaya—to climb peaks that had never been climbed before? Naturally I was nearly mad with excitement when I was asked to join the Gangotri Glacier Expedition in 1933. The leader was my friend Marco Pallis, the well-known explorer.

Snowdon is 3,560 feet in height; I had climbed peaks in the Alps of 13,000 or 14,000 feet; now I was to be amongst mountains that rose to 23,000 feet or more. What a marvellous adventure for a man of twenty-two!

The Gangotri Glacier is one of the main sources of the sacred River Ganges and lies in the centre of the Himalaya, about 500 miles from Everest, the highest mountain in the world. That is not a great distance, when you consider that the Himalaya are over 1,400 miles in length.

The glacier was practically unexplored, and none of the neighbouring peaks had been climbed. It was a prospect too thrilling for words.

Even the voyage was a terrific adventure to me.

We sailed on the *Custodian*, a cargo boat belonging to the Harrison Line. We were the only passengers aboard.

The genial Captain O'Connor amused us with a host of stories. He told us that monkeys could speak if they wanted, but they were afraid that they would be made to work if they did.

Then, talking about earthquakes in South America : The people see the houses bending, but don't worry, because they know they will straighten themselves out.

Manx cats have no tails because they arrived late in the Ark and had the door slammed on them.

Retrievers steer by their tails, and if you cut them off they run round and round in circles.

It was wonderful going south, with the weather getting warmer and warmer. We were kept quite busy with making plans and studying Hindustani and surveying. Still, it seemed very restful after the strain of the hectic final preparations. In the previous month I had seldom got to bed before 2 a.m.

We did a great deal of sunbathing. Marco walked about the hot iron decks barefoot, to get his feet hardened, and one of the Lascars asked him sympathetically if he hadn't got any shoes.

When we had passed Gibraltar and saw the snowy peaks of the Atlas Mountains, over a hundred miles away, seemingly floating on air, our thoughts turned with longing to our much greater goal. It was fascinating to watch the flying fish, and at night the foam round the ship was a mass of sparkling and gleaming phosphorescence.

I wish I had the space to tell you more about the voyage, but I must get on with the real business. We reached Calcutta on 30th April and stayed there only one night. It was all very strange and interesting, my first visit to the East.

The next thrill was seeing the foothills of the Himalaya from the train. They rise suddenly out of the plains to a height of 6,000 to 8,000 feet, though they don't look it. They are partly wooded and partly grassy.

We stayed for a week at Mussoorie, a hill-station at about 6,000 feet, making final arrangements and collecting our porters. We were held up for some time because the local banks had a holiday of several days and we were unable to get any money. This all had to be in small change, since the more primitive natives would not accept notes ; they did not know what they were. £250 worth of money weighed over 50 pounds.

We had some terrible weather whilst we were staying at Mussoorie—hail and thunder and torrential rain. It was cold, too—not at all as I had imagined India to be.

There were five of us in the party—Marco Pallis, Richard Nicholson, Ted Hicks, Dr. Charles Warren, and myself. The first three were very good at Hindustani and even at Tibetan, a very difficult language, but Charles and I were no linguists.

We finally started off on 10th May, with seventy

porters. They each carried loads of 50 pounds. We ourselves carried rucksacks weighing over 35 pounds, although we had been warned that the coolies would despise us if we carried anything at all. As it turned out they respected us all the more for it.

The trek was very hard work, but very interesting. It was terribly hot at first—anything up to 100 degrees in the shade (and there wasn't much shade). Our shoulders got sore from the sacks and we suffered a good deal from thirst. We had to boil all water before it was fit to drink, otherwise we might have got cholera or dysentry or some other unpleasant disease.

After a few days the good exercise began to have its effect, and we felt splendidly fit. We used to walk from ten to fifteen miles each day, sometimes ascending thousands of feet on to high ridges, and then going down again into deep valleys.

After four days we descended to the Ganges. We were below 3,000 feet here, and it was very hot and sticky. We had to eat chocolate with a spoon, and when we opened a tin of butter—almost everything we had was tinned—the butter squirted up in a fountain.

The river flowed through a deep valley. Everything was damp and steamy and there seemed to be no air. It felt rather like the inside of a greenhouse. The slopes on either side were covered with small palms, and there were swarms of monkeys playing about.

At night the place was about as quiet as Euston Station on a bank holiday. Even the thundering of the river failed to drown the squeaking and scraping of the crickets and grasshoppers, to mention only two of the weird sounds.

We went through forests of bamboo and then, as we got higher, came to a magnificent gorge. The walls on either side were vertical for several thousand feet ; their tops were powdered with snow.

We stayed a couple of days at a lovely spot called Harsil, about 8,000 feet above sea-level. Although the temperature was over 70 in the shade, there were several large snow-drifts round about. In one of these there was a 100-foot tunnel, through which I was able to walk.

We changed our porters here and took on a crew of Tibetans, Jadhs (half-Tibetan), and other hill-folk. They could stand the cold and altitude better than the Indians.

Harsil is largely inhabited by Tibetans, and six of them gave a dance in our honour. They made slow and heavy movements with their hands and feet and sang weird tunes. It was all rather impressive and the dancers looked very picturesque, with their bodies made thick and stocky with layers and layers of ragged clothing. Some of the shawls were rather beautiful. The local Chief Lama was present—a delightful little old man, with a wisp of a beard, almond eyes, and a Dutch-looking cap.

After Harsil the scenery grew more and more grand. Only a mountaineer can realize my feelings when I saw the great snowy peaks all round, glittering needles of ice, soaring up into the intense blue of the sky.

The path ended at Gangotri (10,000 feet). It was another nineteen miles to the glacier, over the rough stony bed of the river. Gangotri is a very holy place, since it is the nearest village to the source of the sacred Ganges river. Thousands of pilgrims come here every year, many of them having to walk for hundreds of miles. We saw some very good examples of henpecked husbands—unfortunate pilgrims carrying their wives in baskets on their backs. Perhaps they get used to this sort of thing after a few years of married life.

At the temple at Gangotri red caste-marks were put on our foreheads, and we were given some holy food to eat; it tasted like fudge—threepence a quarter. We hoped it wouldn't give us cholera.

The rest of the way was a wild stony waste. Here and there we were able to cross the river by great snow-bridges, still remaining from the winter. The scenery was superb. Most of the surrounding mountains were not only unclimbed, but even unmarked on the map.

On 25th May, fifteen days after leaving Mussoorie, we reached the Birchwood Camp (12,500 feet), our last camp before the glacier itself and also the last place near any firewood.

We now had to establish our Base Camp on the Gangotri Glacier. I will try to give you some idea of what a Himalayan glacier is like. You will be very wide of the mark if you imagine that it looks like a frozen river. Actually we could not see any ice at all ; the lower part of the glacier was covered with stones and dust—moraine, it is called—for ten miles. When we were actually on the glacier we found that the surface was made up of steep mounds, each about 100 feet in height. These mounds were composed of a thin layer of stones, resting on ice. You can imagine what it was like to walk over them. The stones slipped under your feet, you slipped down and bruised yourself and lost your temper, and everything seemed to be against you.

As soon as we reached the top of one mound we would see an endless array ahead. They all looked exactly the same. So down the other side we would slide, then stumble up the next one—on and on, up and down, up and down—would it never end ?

To establish the Base Camp took us two days with seventeen porters. We had a little trouble with them. We were keeping four to stay with us on the glacier, and these had been given boots and goggles. One of them was proudly wearing his boots, so the others said they wouldn't come on unless they had boots and goggles too. In my best Hindustani I said, " No work, no pay ! " and took off my goggles to show that they weren't necessary. They went on then, after ten minutes' rest for a smoke, and I was able to put on my goggles again when they had forgotten the whole affair.

A HIMALAYAN BIVOUAC.

Camp 2 (19,500 feet) on the Central Satopanth Peak (22,060 feet). Ice-axes are used as
poles for the 4-by-6-foot tent.

THE EFFECTS OF ALTITUDE.

F. E. Hicks at 21,000 feet.

A little farther on one of the older porters collapsed with mountain-sickness (caused by lack of oxygen in the air at this height), and I had the pleasure of feeling what it was like to carry a load of 50 or 60 pounds up a slippery slope of stones and ice at 13,000 feet. The thin thongs dug wickedly into my shoulder and I was very glad to dump it at the top of the steep part.

The Base Camp was at a height of about 14,000 feet. We were not able to find a site at the side that was free from falling stones, so we had to camp right in the middle of the glacier, which was about a mile wide at this point. We had to make level places by clearing away the tops of some of the moraine mounds, pulling up boulders and filling up the holes in the ice with grit. As the ice melted, day by day, great hollows would appear beneath the ground-sheet.

There were two tents on one mound and the other three were about fifty yards away; we couldn't find a place for them any nearer.

Try and imagine the scene. We were surrounded by a desert of dirty-looking stony humps. They looked bleak and ugly, like a vast colliery tip. Here and there were desolate patches of snow, which melted later on. But the mountains on either side more than made up for the miserable foreground. To the east was the great ridge of the Satopanth Group, rising to 23,000 feet. The peaks were sharp and bold, with immense precipices and gleaming bulges of ice, crowned by slopes of dazzling snow that looked too high up to be real.

But it was to the west that our eyes continually turned. There was the mountain that we called the " Matterhorn Peak," after its small brother in the Alps. It was a fearsome yellow tooth of a mountain, rising to 22,000 feet. Smooth rocks rose giddily up ; it was a strain to look so high. The peak narrowed almost to a point. Perched on top of this was an ice-cap—fully 500 feet of vertical ice. It was a breathtaking sight, the savage glaring yellow rock, rising to this delicate and remote summit of ice. We could hardly believe our eyes when we first saw it. I cannot imagine anything more unclimbable. My idea of a mountaineering nightmare is to find myself stuck on those smooth merciless yellow slabs, with avalanches of ice showering down on to me—as they probably would.

So there we were, surrounded by unclimbed mountains. At last my dreams were coming true. What adventures lay ahead of us !

Chapter XV

PIONEER WORK IN THE HIMALAYA

I AM not going to give you a very detailed history of our adventures on the Gangotri Glacier. Quite enough has been written about them already. I just want to give you some idea of the wonderful things that we saw among these virgin peaks, and of my feelings and sensations.

We rose in the mornings at times varying from 4.30 a.m. to 8 o'clock. At a high camp it usually took a couple of hours to get off—sometimes longer. We carried rucksacks weighing from 25 to 30 pounds apiece. This load included the tent, sleeping-bags, spare clothes, cooking apparatus, and food—perhaps a week's supply. As you can imagine, it was no easy job to keep the weight down to reasonable proportions.

Our food at the Base Camp was quite varied, but when we were out attacking a peak it had to be cut down to the lowest possible limit. The mainstay of our diet was pemmican, a very concentrated beef extract, which we made up as a soup. With it we ate dry biscuits. We had pemmican in the morning and evening only; the rest of the day we lived on boiled sweets. These are very good on account of the sugar they contain, which gives you energy very quickly. We used to keep a good supply in our pockets, so that we could eat without having to stop.

I think the best thing for me to do is to give you an account of a typical three-days' climb up a 20,000-foot peak on the west of the glacier. I had already done two fairly easy peaks, one of them about 18,000 feet high. This was a mere midget here, of course, although 2,000 feet higher than Mont Blanc, the highest mountain in the Alps.

Teddie Hicks and I set off from the Base Camp at midday on 3rd June. We first had to cross the main glacier, where we had some bother in getting round a lake, which lay in an icy basin.

Our peak rose above a side glacier, which we eventually reached after many unpleasant surprises in the shape of a swampy valley half-filled with snow, a river, and a long scree-slope.

The glacier was terrible. The sun was burning down on us and the snow was soft and slushy. We sank in to our knees and grew more and more tired. It got worse. We sank up to our waists. We didn't speak at all, except to swear. There was no sign of a camp site.

We crossed to the right of the glacier, but it was no better there. There were some small crevasses about, but we didn't bother to rope. We were almost past caring what happened to us.

At last we reached a moraine ridge, which gave us quite a smooth path for a long way. At 4 o'clock, when we were nearly 16,000 feet, we decided to camp.

There was very little room, but we cleared the stones off the top of the ridge and managed to make enough space. Our tent was 4 feet by 6, and 3 feet high. It weighed about a couple of pounds. The ground-sheet was sewn in, and we used ice-axes as poles. There were four guy-lines—one at each end and another two to pull out the sides. We used no tent-pegs, but put stones on the guys and on the special flap provided round the outside of the tent. The door was a wide sleeve, through which you had to crawl. It could then be tied up, so that no snow or cold air could get in.

The first thing to do was to cook our " dinner " on the primus stove. To get any water, of course, we had to melt snow. Two pints of snow make about a cupful of water, so the whole process is a great waste of paraffin. Then we put in the pemmican and added some soup powder to give it a fresh flavour. We put in a different kind of soup every time, but the flavour was always the same— pemmican.

We had some chocolate biscuits as well and got into our sleeping-bags at 5.15. Our sleeping-bags were made of eiderdown, an outer one with a hood and zip-fastener, so that it could be closed right over the face if necessary, and an inner one that came just up to the neck. We found that they kept us quite warm in 32 degrees of frost, although they weighed only 4½ pounds complete.

It was a wonderful night—so wonderful that we kept the door open. We were just opposite the great north face of the Matterhorn Peak—7,000 feet of it. We could see the two peaks now, sticking up like fearsome fangs against the evening sky. The rock went deep red, and the icy summit a delicate pink. The shadow crept up and everything was dark except for the scarlet flush where the sinking sun still touched the final ice-cap.

Presently the moon rose and made the scene even more exquisitely beautiful. The snow-slopes looked dream-like and ghostly where they curved down into the glacier bed, but the towering rocks still looked bold and black and strong.

We got up at 4.30, poured our breakfast of pemmican out of the thermos—horrible !—and got away by 5 o'clock, the earliest start of the expedition.

We started up a snow-slope, which we hoped would lead us right up to the ridge of our peak. The snow was hard, and we put on our crampons. Before long Teddie lost all feeling in one of his feet. He was beginning to get frostbite ; the tight crampon straps had stopped the circulation. There was nothing for it but to take off the boot and rub the foot for half an hour, when feeling returned. If you take a thing like this in time there is no danger ; neglect it and you may lose all your toes.

At 7 o'clock we came to steep rocks and roped-up. The climbing soon became very difficult. We were not yet acclimatized—used to the height, that is—

and the effort of climbing up an overhang completely exhausted us.

Some of you may not know why things become more difficult at a great height. If you sprint for a hundred yards you get puffed and breathless. Why ? Because your body runs on oxygen, and if you make an extra effort you need an extra supply of oxygen. It is in order to obtain this extra supply that you breathe more rapidly. Now, at 20,000 feet there is only about half the amount of oxygen in the air that there is at sea-level. The air is altogether thinner. Therefore you have to breathe more quickly to get enough oxygen. So you get very breathless just walking slowly uphill. It would be quite impossible to run for any distance.

Oxygen also supplies heat to the body, so when you are high up you feel the cold and get frostbite much more easily. The brain and all the digestive organs also depend on oxygen, so you also find it hard to think and lose your appetite and often feel sick. The whole business is a great strain on the heart.

Now, if you were suddenly taken up to 20,000 feet, without a cylinder of oxygen, you would probably be very sick and ill, and might even die if your heart wasn't sound. You certainly wouldn't be fit to do any work. Yet how is it that on Everest people have been able not only to keep alive, but also to climb, at an altitude of over 28,000 feet ? The answer is that after being high up for a few weeks you begin to get acclimatized; that is, you get used to the conditions. The blood changes, so that you can work on less oxygen. It is still very exhausting to take any exertion, but you can do it. After a time the strain begins to tell and your condition becomes worse. Therefore, it is for only a short time that you are at your best.

We hadn't had sufficient time to get properly acclimatized ; that is why we found the overhang so very exhausting. It would have been difficult enough at sea-level ; here it took us several minutes to get our breath back again.

Things became a little easier after that, but the whole slope was very steep. All the ledges were covered with "sea-foam" snow. This was about two feet deep and looked and felt like frozen soap-suds. I believe it is to be found only in tropical districts. It is very beautiful, but tiring and dangerous to climb on.

We felt very exhausted at 10.30, so we had an hour's rest and made some tea, after which we felt much better.

We reached the top of the rocks and came to a snow-slope. It wasn't very steep, but it was soft and wet. We sank in to our knees, then to our waists. Each step was a ghastly effort. My head swam and I felt ill and dreadfully weak. How much more ? My 30-pound rucksack seemed to be dragging me backwards. I just wanted to lie down in the snow and stay there for ever.

We took half an hour over 200 feet of this stuff. It seemed like half a day. We pitched camp—about

AN UNCLIMBED HIMALAYAN GIANT.
The 22,000-foot " Matterhorn Peak," from our 19,000-foot
camp.

19,000 feet—at 2.15 p.m. The snow was quite deep and we had to cut out a level platform. With our axes we hewed away a foot of snow and then a foot of ice. It was terribly exhausting. Every few minutes I would drop down, gasping, on to the wet snow. At this height you don't bother to sit down ; you just fall down. On our previous expedition I had gone much better than Teddie Hicks ; this time he was by far the fresher. Yet a fortnight later, when I was more acclimatized, I felt fairly comfortable at 22,000 feet, on the summit of the Central Satopanth Peak. I never felt well between 19,000 and 21,000 feet. Above that height I seemed to improve. I cannot explain why this should be, but other climbers have noticed the same kind of thing, though not always at the same height.

It had been a trying and difficult day. No one had even attempted the mountain before, so we had no idea whether it was possible or whether we were on the best route. Yet this is the part of it that makes all the hardships worth while. There is all the excitement of being where no man has ever been before ; there is the interest of the route finding and the difficulty of the climbing. There is an urge that sends you on and makes you feel that no effort is too great.

The Matterhorn Peak looked magnificently imposing. From this height we could see it in its true proportions. It appeared to be nearly vertical on all sides—a twisted monster of white and yellow, but with a strange and dreadful attraction.

While we were climbing we had not noticed the view. You cannot appreciate any kind of beauty when you are feeling weak and distressed.

I will let my diary tell the story of the remainder of the climb :

We fed inside the tent. I found pemmican sickening at this height ; I spilt some over my fur collar and smelt it all night. We did not undress to go to bed, but instead put on two extra sweaters. I took two soda mints and two aspirins and slept quite well.

The temperature fell to 24 degrees below freezing, and all the inside of the tent was covered with frost. The sleeping-bags were stiff with ice round our mouths. We had the entrance open and I kept quite warm, though my feet got cold in the morning, through being against the end of the tent.

Up at 5 a.m. and then back to bed again to melt my boots, which I had left uncovered in the tent. They were so stiff that it was quite impossible to get them on. I nursed them in my sleeping-bag for over an hour before they showed any signs of softening, and even when I did get them on my toes froze straight away.

For breakfast we had the remains of last night's pemmican, which we had put into a thermos. I always felt sick in the mornings when high up, and this pemmican was just about the last straw.

First a thin yellow liquid came out. This was followed by lumps of what looked like thick brown mud. We took it as a medicine, because we knew it was good for us.

It began to snow heavily, and thick cloud came down. We finally got up at 7—after breakfast in bed—what luxury!—and packed everything up, intending to descend. A miserable business. Suddenly the mist began to break, so we determined to have a shot at our peak.

We set off at 7.30, without rucksacks. I felt terribly weak and had to rest every few feet. Ted had to cut most of the steps, but I managed to do the last hundred feet or so to the top, in hard snow. I would cut five steps, with two breaths to every step, and then rest, leaning on my axe or collapsing in the snow. Not an atom of enjoyment. We reached the summit (about 20,100 feet) at 10.30 a.m. We felt no sense of exhilaration—just thank goodness that's over. Thick cloud—snowing off and on. A snow summit, with a few stones about— also two spiders, poor devils! We hadn't the energy to build a cairn.

We stayed on top only ten minutes. I felt dreadful going down through the soft snow to the tent, which we reached in about an hour. We packed up and had some food and water here. Then we discovered that we had left our sweaters some 200 feet higher up, so Teddie gallantly reascended and recovered them.

We continued down. As soon as we reached the rocks I felt very much better, and we went for hours without a rest. It was rather dangerous ground—

loose snow on all the ledges. We abseiled down the
very difficult pitch and then did a sitting glissade
down a snow-slope of avalanche débris—very wet
and bumpy. We both got bad headaches, as we
always did when descending.

We reached the site of our lower camp at
3.30 p.m. and continued down. It was snowing
quite a lot. Thank goodness we weren't still
camped up above ! It would be terrible in this
weather. It was marvellous to be down again,
where one felt alive and things seemed real.

There was some fiendish snow on the glacier.
We reached Base Camp at 5.30 p.m. Not so very
tired. Warm night. Rained quite a lot. Bed
7.30 p.m.

This was not a very important peak ; it wasn't
even the highest point on the ridge. But I have
chosen to tell you about it for two reasons. Firstly,
I don't think the ascent has ever before been
described in print ; secondly, it was my first visit
to 20,000 feet, and I suffered more from the altitude
than at any other time ; so it is a useful example
for describing the effects of oxygen shortage.

You can read about the rest of the expedition
in Marco Pallis's book, *Peaks and Lamas*, so I will
give just a brief summary.

Two other 20,000-foot peaks were climbed, and
then three of us were turned back on a peak we
called the Great Snow Mountain, or the Great
White Lump. We also called it other things, not

so polite. It was about 22,000 feet, and we took skis up to 19,000 feet. It was a dull mountain—days of heartbreaking slopes of snow and ice—and a snowstorm finally forced us to retreat when we were only 500 feet below the summit, but getting rather short of food.

The Central Satopanth Peak (22,060 feet) took us six days. It was a very difficult rock peak, and we had five camps actually on the mountain and narrowly escaped being marooned by the monsoon.

Two of us had to return home after that, and Pallis and Warren climbed the isolated peak of Riwo Pargyul (22,210 feet), on the borders of Tibet.

I don't believe that any one, at the time, can really enjoy being high up on a Himalayan peak. There is the urge that makes you go on ; there is the satisfaction you feel after a successful climb. Then there is the awe-inspiring scenery ; only the climber can enjoy this to the full. He is in tune with the mountains. You feel these things and decide to climb the mountain. But high up all pleasure disappears. You push on because, when you were down in the valley, you made up your mind to push on. And when you get down again you are glad that you have not given in.

I suppose the natural human urge for adventure is at the bottom of it all. The hundreds of unclimbed peaks in the Himalaya will satisfy that urge for a long time to come.

CHAPTER XVI

GOOD-BYE AND GOOD LUCK

I FEEL, now, that I know you quite well. I have started you off on the best of all pastimes, and I am quite sure that you will do me credit.

Some of you may feel that you will never have the nerve or skill to do the hardest climbs ; in such a case you may wonder whether it is worth your while to start at all. My answer to that is a definite yes. You will get just as much pleasure if you never do anything more than difficult. Your main object in climbing should be enjoyment, not achievement. You may feel, as I have felt, that you must try harder and harder climbs. You will certainly get more kick out of it that way, and I wish you every success. But if you feel quite happy on the easier climbs and have no wish to go further, don't get discouraged and think yourself a failure. Just find your own standard and stick to it.

You would expect that when I returned from the Himalaya I would find the Welsh hills very uninteresting. Not a bit of it. It was like meeting old friends after a long absence. I had a lot of lectures to give, and a lot of articles to write, so that I was pretty busy for a time. But I seized every possible opportunity of getting down to my beloved Wales. At first I did not want to try anything very difficult. In the Himalaya, of course, a difficult pitch was an enemy, that wasted valuable time and energy. It was a little while before I could get myself accustomed to looking for difficulty. My natural tendency was to find the easiest way up a mountain.

I have been able to give you only a rather sketchy idea of what you need to know, especially about Alpine climbing. I haven't told you anything about winter climbing in the Alps, which involves ski-ing and is really a separate sport. I don't know enough about it to be able to speak with authority. But I think you will find that I have told you all you need to know about rock-climbing. For the Alps you will need an experienced companion in any case ; I have just tried to give you some idea of what the climbing there is like.

When you get really keen, you cannot do better than read *Mountain Craft*, by Geoffrey Winthrop Young, which is the classic on mountaineering technique. Girls, who will like to know what can be done by women climbers, should get hold of *Climbing Days*, by Dorothy Pilley, which is full of the exciting adventures of that brilliant lady mountaineer.

Some of the climbing clubs have huts or cottages in Wales or the Lakes. Here you can enjoy a week-end or a long holiday right away from every-day life. Everything is very free and easy. You do your own cooking and sleep on bunks, rather like those in an Alpine hut. When you first come in, you will think what an extraordinary crowd the others look. Some have just arrived and are in city clothes. Others are in ragged climbing clothes, their big boots in every one's way. But nobody minds ; you just do as you like here. A steaming curtain of wet clothes hangs in front of the fire. The owners are lolling about in pyjamas or old football jerseys and shapeless flannel trousers.

The plain wooden table is strewn with all kinds of weird dishes. This is a grand place to experiment in cooking. I once ran out of dripping, and made some excellent fried bread in vaseline.

The whole place looks in a terrible state of confusion and untidiness. Then comes the grand wash-up, and order is once more restored. Everything is spick and span—except the climbers themselves. You get things done properly when you haven't got any women messing about.

In Wasdale, however, the Fell and Rock Climbing Club has a splendid hut, which accommodates climbers of both sexes.

Some of the Youth Hostels, also, are very well situated for climbing, notably Idwal Cottage, in the Ogwen Valley, which is one of the best.

You will find that climbers are most friendly people, always willing to help a keen novice. You don't need to be introduced when you meet any one on the mountains. You usually say " good-day ! " or " what foul weather it is," or have a chat about some climb.

If you overtake a slower party on a climb it is considered bad manners to try to pass them unless they ask you to. Actually they usually will do so, and you should do the same if you are holding up another party.

You will have gathered that there is just as much humour as adventure in climbing. I remember a very curious meal I once had on the top of Ben Nevis. It was a cold Easter, and two friends of ours were camping inside the old observatory, so Alf Bridge and I decided we would join them for supper. The only item on the menu was porridge. We didn't use plates; we just dipped into the saucepan. We didn't complain about that. But the porridge was very thin, and our two generous hosts had provided themselves with spoons, while Alf and I had to manage as best we could with forks.

One Sunday I was climbing a little 50-foot problem at Helsby, suitably called the Overhanging Crack. I reached the top and then quietly descended by an easy route to the foot of the cliff. I had arranged the rope so that it came up from my second, over an edge of rock and down to me, so that I had him quite safely held. Then I pulled in the rope and my second began to climb up. Just when he was having a lot of difficulty with the overhang I gave a shout. Hearing my voice come from below him, the poor man nearly fell off with fright. He thought that I had unroped and left him to his fate.

If you keep your eyes open you will find quite

a lot of little cliffs where you can taste some of the
joys of exploring. But beware of rotten rock ;
limestone is especially bad in this respect. Sea-cliffs
are not usually good, but the Cornish coast provides
some excellent climbing. Quite a lot of exploration
has been done here, but much is still untouched.
Some of the routes are over 200 feet in height. The
rock is rougher than anything you will get in Wales
or the Lakes—firm steep granite, like the Chamonix
Aiguilles. Many of the climbs, in fact, seem like
small editions of these famous Alpine pinnacles ;
only, instead of tumbled glaciers, you have the
rolling sea below you.

In Yorkshire and Derbyshire there are many
small cliffs of gritstone—a rock something like
sandstone, but very much harder and more reliable.
These are very popular, and are well-placed for
any one living in Manchester or Sheffield. I have
purposely not mentioned them before, since they
require a special technique of their own. There
are many climbers who are brilliant on gritstone,
and yet cannot do anything on ordinary rock.
Severe though many of them are, these gritstone
climbs are not a very important part of mountaineering. So I advise you to leave them alone until you
have got a good groundwork on real mountains.
Then you will find gritstone a great help in im-
proving your standard.

Whether you turn out to be daring experts on
the British crags or the great ice-faces of the Alps
and Himalaya, or whether you are content to potter

about on the easy climbs, I wish you the very best of luck. I hope I shall meet some of you on the hills.

If mountaineering gives you half as much pleasure as it has given me, you will never regret having taken it up.

INDEX

INDEX

PRINTED IN GREAT BRITAIN AT
THE PRESS OF THE PUBLISHERS